THE WISDOM OF FOOLS?

Also by Mary Grey and published by SPCK:

*Redeeming the Dream: Feminism, Redemption
and Christian Tradition* (1989)

Mary Grey

THE WISDOM OF FOOLS?

Seeking Revelation for Today

First published in Great Britain 1993
Society for Promoting Christian Knowledge
Holy Trinity Church
Marylebone Road
London NW1 4DU

© Mary Grey 1993

British Library Cataloguing-in-Publication Data

A catalogue record for this book is available
from the British Library

ISBN 0-281-04659-X

Typeset and printed in Great Britain by
The Longdunn Press Ltd, Bristol

Hidden God,
Whose wisdom compels our love
and unsettles all our values;
fill us with desire
to search for her truth,
that we may transform the world
becoming fools for her sake,
through Jesus Christ, Amen.

Janet Morley, *All Desires Known*

The Holy fool is 'the wanderer or pilgrim who feels equally at
home everywhere, yet settles down nowhere. Clothed in rags
even in the winter cold . . . he renounces not only material
possessions but also what others regard as his sanity and
mental balance. Yet thereby he becomes a channel for the
higher wisdom of the Spirit.

Kallistos Ware, *The Orthodox Way*

The moment for the birth of the spiritual child is now at hand,
and the travail of childbirth becomes intense. Grace, the
common mother of us all, hastens to give birth mystically to
the soul, God's image, bringing it forth into the light of the
Age to come.

St Isaac the Syrian, *Mystic Treatises*

Everything that is in the heavens, on the earth, and under the
earth is penetrated with connectedness, penetrated with
relatedness.

Hildegarde of Bingen

Contents

Foreword   ix

Introduction   1

1   *Seeking the Right Question*   5

2   *Woman: Silent Outsider to Revelation*   14

3   *Living the Sacrifice and the Lost Experience of Women*   30

INTERMEZZO: Cassandra, Voice from the Margins

4   *Connectedness as New Metaphor for Christian Revelation*   57

5   *The Separate Self and the Denial of Relation*   67

6   *Revelation and Connected Knowing*   81

7   *The Fragility of Divine Communication*   93

8   *God and Evil within a Metaphysic of Connection*   101

9   *The Church: Permanently Marginal, or Leaven for Change?*   120

10   *A Revelation Story for our Times?*   137

Notes   145

Index   161

Foreword

The life-experience behind this book has been my husband Nicholas's and my own involvement and commitment to a project to build wells in a drought-stricken area of Rajasthan, India. I have had to ask the whole time: What relevance does Christian theology have to problems on such a huge scale? I am indebted to Nicholas for his practical reactions to my (theoretical) questions, which kept me alert to the evasions and inadequacies of the theological answers. Another part of the background has been my teaching work in the University of Nijmegen, The Netherlands: I would like to thank the students of 'Feminisme en Christendom' for the lively discussions over the last three years as well as my friends and colleagues in feminist theology in England, The Netherlands – in fact in many countries in Europe – and, increasingly, in other parts of the world. 'Connection Theology' has, in a very real way, developed in response to the discussions with all of you and the problems we have faced together. I am grateful to Annelies van Heijst (the Netherlands) and Anne Primavesi (England) for their comments on parts of this text and to Judith Longman (SPCK) for continually supporting my efforts. I would like to dedicate this book to my mother, the first image of Sophia I encountered, who remained, until the time of her recent death, an unfailing source of loving wisdom for her children and grandchildren.

Mary Grey
February 1992

Introduction

The real reason why I wanted to write a book about revelation *now* is, above all, because this is a time of revelation.

Since the fall of the Berlin Wall in 1989 we have lived in political and social upheaval. The philosophical upheaval pre-dated this, but has received a new impetus in its wake. I am convinced that the old analysis of culture, politics and religion is breaking up and that this presents a unique moment for understanding the relationship between God and world. Culture is cracking – but what will fill the cracks?

I have become convinced that feminist theology should not follow blindly the pre-ordained headings of a traditional systematic theology of revelation – God/Christ/Spirit/Church/eschatology, and so on. Rather, the only way to new understanding is for contemporary religious faith to grope for answers *by better understanding the questions*. That I am able to do this at all is because of the changes on the theological scene of the last twenty-five years. Without the Dogmatic Constitution of the Second Vatican Council on revelation, *Dei Verbum* (November 1965), the immense task of understanding changing human experience and culture in the light of Scripture and tradition would not have taken off so rapidly – in the Roman Catholic Church, at least. We have been flooded with new attempts to understand revelation and experience, revelation and history, revelation and culture, revelation and liberation. But there have been no theologies of revelation written by women.

In order not to fall automatically into a pre-arranged pattern, but rather to see revelation within a theology of mutual relation, as divine communication for our times, the 'filter' through which we understand our culture, our identity, and how we relate to the world of the sacred must be brought to light. I see us as balanced between two myths, or ways of receiving the world. 'Myth' is used here as a symbolic narrative through which we give our experience coherence, and relate to past, present and future. In contrast with some contemporary thinkers, I do not make a sharp contrast between mythic and historical thinking. Myths themselves originate as response to a particular context and culture. As human beings we are always myth-makers, as interpreters of our own culture.

What I have searched for is a way to allow the two myths of our time to be in dialogue with each other. The dominant myth is the logo-centric, profit-based, competitive ethic of the richer countries of the northern hemisphere. This I have personified in the character of *Logos*. The second myth underlies and is almost submerged by the dominant culture: it is non-dualistic, non-competitive, ecological and relational. I have personified this in the character of *Sophia*. I believe the dominant understanding of Christian revelation is too controlled by the Logos myth. It is this which imposes a tight control on 'truth' and 'truths'. It is this which keeps in being the dominant understanding of God as a ruling male, and Christ as the (male) high point of the whole of creation, reducing the Spirit to an anaemic dove symbol. It is this which keeps the Christian Church imprisoned in a 'fortress Falklands' mentality, its ecumenical endeavours stifled in a monolithic model of vertical, hierarchical unity.

But two warnings are needed. First, I am not making a crude identification of men with Logos, and women with Sophia. The Logos culture involves both men and women in different ways, in its ways of operation, decision-making and power structures. The inclusive vision of Sophia is an invitation to the whole of creation to live according to different patterns. Second, I do not condemn technology through a plea to return to 'pure nature'; nor do I condemn Logos/reason/rationality in favour of a romantic opting-out of culture. It is a *particular interpretation* of Logos and the exclusive consequences of its operation which is being explored through this story.

To bring these two myths into tension with each other I have introduced a third character, *Perceval*. I have called him the Holy Fool, although I know that, according to legend and history, he was a Knight of the Holy Grail.

Many strands come together in this figure. I am recalling Harvey Cox's evocation, in *The Feast of Fools*, of that medieval colourful feast (not beloved of the powers that be) where

2

the Lord of Misrule, a Mock King, a Boy Bishop was elected to preside over the events . . . During the Feast of Fools no custom or convention was immune to ridicule and even the highest personages of the realm could expect to be lampooned.[1]

Perceval as the Holy Fool can move throughout history, free to make fun of institutions, and to ask questions. Perceval is also the Holy Fool in the sense of the youngest son in the legends. It is he who must seek his fortune without the benefit of wealth and parental favour. His 'happy ending' is achieved through sheer guilelessness, 'holy innocence' – by listening to animals and birds and the wise woman.[2] It is in this sense that he evokes the words of Jesus, 'I thank thee, Father, Lord of Heaven and earth, that thou hast hidden these things from the wise and understanding and revealed them to babes' (Matt. 11.25) as well as the words of Paul 'We are fools for Christ's sake' (1 Cor. 4.10).

So in Perceval I recognize something of the innocent child, and see clearly culture's need to image deity as divine child.

I also see Perceval as a deeply Christian figure, who shows that the revelation of Christianity is capable of being understood in different ways. What questions we bring to our reading of revelation is of crucial significance for the achieving of justice in the world.

The question I bring to Christian revelation is, How can revelation be understood in such a way as to bring God's justice to the victims of global oppression? How can it address the catastrophic situation of the planet, at what might be understood as the eleventh hour of life on earth? To do this I will interweave story and theological argument. If readers find the story interrupts the argument, simply leave it and turn to the argument. But I believe and hope that the story expresses something which the reasoned argument could not. So I will begin by a confrontation between Logos and Sophia, to introduce some of the problems encountered in the traditional understanding of Christian revelation (chapter 1). Second, I will highlight the position of women, outsiders to revelation, and show how current models of revelation are inadequate when examined from a Christian feminist point of view (chapter 2). Chapter 3 then tries to discover what is lost from revelation by excluding the experience of women. What has happened and is happening to the experience of women within patriarchal Christianity? An 'Intermezzo' is then presented: How does the prophetic voice of Cassandra, princess of Troy, condemned as mad by the verdict of tradition, offer any insights to the lost experience?

In chapters 4 and 5 I explore the promise of a metaphor of connectedness as a prism through which to understand revelation, followed by the search for a new way of coming to know, recognize and integrate our experience, the way of 'connected knowing' (chapter 6). Here we again encounter Perceval, Logos and Sophia – this time in Greece, one famous source of philosophical wisdom, for Europe at least. Chapter 7 asks how we could then look at Christian tradition, given the prism of a metaphysic of connection.

In chapters 8 and 9 I face the two most difficult questions of 'connection theology', namely, on an organic, connected world-view how do we understand the relationship between God and evil (chapter 8)? Second, where is this theology of connection to be encountered and expressed? Is it to be condemned to remain permanently on the margins of society? Could it not contribute to a theology of Church (chapter 9)? Finally, I return to Perceval and ask him to confront the distortions of his own story anew. With him, we read with new eyes a text of Christian revelation which offers new hope for 'Apocalypse now' (chapter 10).

1 Seeking the Right Question

A DIALOGUE BETWEEN TWO MYTHS

This chapter sets the scene. What is the specific context in which Christian faith seeks anew to understand divine revelation? What questions should be posed to elicit a new understanding? To challenge the presuppositions and assumptions in western society we need a character who, to some extent, stands outside our culture, a character who can poke fun at the empty power games of the privileged and challenge us with new questions. Hence I introduce Perceval, medieval hero of the legends of the Holy Grail.

According to these legends, the Holy Fool, the young boy Perceval, escapes from his weeping mother Herzeloide, seeking adventure and the meaning of existence.[1] Too long has his mother kept him from the grim realities of the outside world. But what he discovers is the total break-up of contemporary culture. The king, Amfortas, lies sick of a mortal wound and his sickness is reflected by the barren earth itself. Because of the failure of fertility, the environment is polluted and nothing grows. The entire civilization is in fragments: it awaits the wisdom of the Holy Fool who can ask the right question and set in motion the healing of land and people.

Perceval's initial failure to ask the right question is mirrored by the cultural crisis which envelops us today. Much of our planet is already irretrievably waste land. As Perceval wanders from the desert of the Sudanese Sahel to the dead waters of the Aral Sea, to contemplate the ravaged forest of the Amazon, despair grips his spirit. The break-up of communist regimes, the unification of Germany and the ending of the Cold War did bring initial euphoria. But these developments have also been accompanied by the growing realization that a deeper cultural break-up underlies them. There is a growing fear that the great systems which gave meaning to the construction of modern civilization – including liberal democracy itself – have

5

themselves been held in the balance and found wanting; *the centre does not hold any more.* The Holy Grail now on offer to these 'liberated' countries is itself short-changed, holding only the competitiveness and profit-oriented values of the market economy. Thus Perceval is equally at a loss as to the right question which will usher in the healing of the planet.

The Holy Fools of myth and legend must always undergo much discipline and purification before they attain the necessary wisdom to pose the relevant question. Perceval of the Grail stories attained the desired state through retreat from the world and the discipline of the hermit Trevrezent. But the Holy Fool today seeks wisdom not in flight, but in open confrontation with the systems, the accepted wisdoms, and the discourses which must take responsibility for the crisis. This he does by entering into dialogue with the 'myths' of the culture. Myth as the story by which we live may be found not only as the official story by which we claim to live – our faith, national and cultural stories – but also, on the level of the symbolic, as the underlying myth which is actually shaping the whole of our cultural and political contexts, at both conscious and unconscious levels.

The Holy Fool will dialogue, through the pages of this book, with two opposing ways of viewing the world. The first will be the Logos myth of nationalistic individualism and materialistic success, which I call the predominant myth of European culture. This has a long and complex history, with philosophical, theological and economic dimensions. (These I will return to later.) The other myth is more difficult to define. It almost eludes grasp. It is more a question of intuiting another story beneath the dominant culture, a story which has been pushed to the margins of consciousness and public responsibility. It is the myth of connectedness, which conveys a sense of rootedness in the earth, with its changing seasons and rhythms, and a sense of interdependence, which sees human beings as vulnerable parts of a wider, interlocking whole, not as 'masters of the universe'. This story has philosophical, theological, political and ethical implications, and it will be the task of this book to spell out some of these. But Perceval must dialogue with both myths.

Imagine the Holy Fool one morning, parking his bicycle

outside a brand new, high-rise office block. Perceval first confronts Logos, installed before a huge computer system in the spacious office of an international daily newspaper, high up in this tall building, with a commanding view over the city. Within easy reach of his fax machine and telephone, Logos is fed with world news minute by minute by flashing news screens in front of him. His multi-lingual staff and instantaneous translating service ensure that no country in the world escapes his attention. Every item of information is related to the share index, the international exchange rate, and checked with the ever-changing relationship between the Pentagon and the Kremlin. The atmosphere is one of infectious excitement: the team is young and dynamic, filled with a conviction that real progress is being accelerated, and a prosperous future being built within these walls. Nor is Logos's attention focused only on the present. Through his computer databank he can contact all the libraries of the world, so that no great event, no world celebrity or disaster remains uncharted or unrelated to its historical antecedent.

Perceval slips away, troubled. He cannot begin to formulate a question, and cycles off into the traffic. By the time he has reached the suburbs of the city, night has fallen and he is weary, both spiritually and physically. Before the city has awoken to the glamour of its night-life, the Holy Fool has made his way into the forest and stumbled across a gipsy encampment.

The night is chilly and a group are huddled together, seeking warmth around the camp-fire. A dark-haired woman is telling tales by its glowing embers. Near her gather both children and old people, poets, musicians, and artists busily crafting pieces of wood or moulding clay. In the flickering firelight a people are remembering, dreaming and grieving. The story-teller is evoking forgotten times when the streams were full of fish, the forests were still luxuriant with insect, bird and animal life, when the workers of the fields brought home plenty to eat. She is grieving for the communities broken up by slave-trader, land-developer or invader, for the lost children sold into slavery or kidnapped into prostitution. She sings of the Great Spirit of their lost past, whose beating wings evoked courage, transcendence and yearning for freedom. Perceval listens, spellbound.

Before dawn she is on her way. As the morning chorus of the

birds fills the air, she makes her way to the town prison. Responding to the loneliness and despair within, she sings of more hopeful times. She connects broken men and women with earlier memories and hopes of freedom. She speaks of the tenderness and love which sustains men and women through suffering, and spins dreams of their homecoming to build new lives. From dawn to dusk through village and market-place she wanders, breaking bread in cottage and tent, sleeping at last under the bridges with homeless young people. But always weaving stories of hidden hopes and lost memories – stories which bind broken people to past and future. At last Perceval recognizes her. She is Sophia, Wisdom, who speaks for those excluded from the onward rush of progress. She, he realizes, has all along been the prompting for his setting out once more on the quest for the Holy Grail.

One morning Logos held a press conference with all the politicians and religious leaders shaping the new Europe's relationship with the wider world. Perceval sat unnoticed in a corner. Logos spoke confidently of the unique promise of this moment in history. He proclaimed the chance of an undreamt-of material prosperity, and was convinced that poorer countries would eventually feel the benefit of this. Though developing technology was bringing temporary job loss, this would be overcome by greater personal initiative and individual enterprise. Churches and religious leaders of all faiths – although they would have to face up to the fact that people would need to turn less to the comforts of religion – would have a crucial role to play in encouraging the moral fibre essential for such achievements.

At this moment Logos paused for breath, and, incredibly, someone intervened. Perceval recognized the voice of Sophia. Although she was speaking, it was as if she sang. In haunting tones, evoking lost memories of nights under the stars, the ancient memory of attending to the rhythms of the universe, and the sensitivity of a deep listening, Sophia challenged the assembly with a vision far more profound than the political programmes being conjured up in this conference chamber.

Logos had also recognized her. 'Sophia,' he shouted angrily, 'your so-called visions are the enemy of progress and culture! Take them to the shanty towns and the backwoods where they

belong! Progress needs hard analysis, not sentimental stories!'
Yet Sophia persisted, her dark eyes with their penetrating
gaze, her energy and fire compelling the reluctant attention of
the politicians. It was a scene to delight the Holy Fool.

'You, Logos,' cried Sophia, 'with your ruthless schemes of
progress – you leave behind those who would live by a different
tune. The prosperity you offer is built on the exploitation of
women and children, on sweeping the misfits to the edges of
society, and on consigning the old and sick to the dustbin of
history! In the name of your progress the garden of our world
is being transformed into desert!' Sophia began rocking, as if
trying to recall the stunned assembly to an archaic, long-
forgotten rhythm. The contrast between the rocking Sophia,
her flowing hair covering her face, and the stiff, grey-suited
executives, embarrassed even the Church leaders present.

'Sophia,' the grey old men began remonstrating, 'we know
it's hard for you, but you had your day and you served your
purpose. We all had to emerge from your primal mythological
chaos; we could not remain forever swimming in your cosmic
soup. Instinct, feeling, oceanic emotion – they must all in the
end cede to reasoned analysis. 'In the Beginning was the
Word', after all!'

At this Sophia rose to her feet and swept her grey cloak
around her shoulders. She was clearly a figure commanding
respect. 'Ah – but behind the word?' she asked. 'And what
word do you utter in the name of progress? And who is
compelled to silence by the word of the consumer society?
Where is the word which tells of beginnings and utters faith in
endings? And what would happen if the voiceless roared into
speech from 'the other side of silence?'[2]

As she swept from the room, for a moment Logos felt a rush
of wings and inhaled the smell of moist pinewoods and the
fragrance of the musk-rose. It was a moment of intense
disappointment for Perceval. Why had Sophia not remained
and persevered with the confrontation? Did this mean she
would have no voice in future negotiations? In a moment of
insight he saw that in the continuing dialogue between these
two lay the moulding of his questions.

As for Logos, he turned briskly to the next item on the
agenda.

9

IN THE BEGINNING – THE HEARING?

Perceval's failure to find the right question, and the inability of Logos to 'hear' Sophia, illustrate sharply the contemporary dilemma. At this moment of time, vanished are the clear certainties which built the culture of modernism. First, the foundations of philosophy, psychology, science and language are all being thrown into the quagmire of post-modernism.[3] The great 'masters of suspicion' – Freud, Nietzsche, Durkheim and Marx – are themselves now subject to suspicion. For beneath political change are hidden deeper philosophical and cultural factors. That great cultural creation, the seamless garment which was the 'Europe of Christendom', exists no more. This was the Europe built on the art of Michelangelo and Rembrandt, the music of Beethoven, the poetry of Shakespeare and Goethe. It was permeated by the Christian faith, forced by fire and sword on Jew and Muslim alike. 'Europe is the Faith and the Faith is Europe', wrote Hilaire Belloc, and hundreds of Gothic cathedrals, spires aiming for the heavens, exist to prove it.[4] But Europe is now multi-faith and multi-cultural: it has become a matrix of overlapping cultures and discourses. Moreover it is conscious that it owes its wealth to the legacy (or piracy) of empire, and is aware, to some degree, of links with poorer parts of the world, for whose entrapment in poverty European exploitation is partially responsible.

Second, the medieval world-view, sharply dividing heaven from earth, divine from human, body from soul, seeing salvation as reward for earthly ethical behaviour, has given way to a much more integrated understanding of holiness, a call to experience 'the beyond in our midst'[5] and to work for the realization of the kingdom of peace and justice in the here-and-now.

Third, the whole understanding of human subjectivity is called into question by the realization that women have not until recently been considered full human subjects – politically, philosophically, psychologically, sexually and theologically – so that analyses of 'mankind' simply do not fit the experience of women as this has begun to be articulated. Women have been considered the objects of history, never its subjects. They have been the 'other' to a masculine norm, lacking access to education, vote and voice. At times even basic human essentials have been beyond their reach.[6]

Hence there is real danger that we construct a new cultural and political synthesis in which the old unjust power-relations and structures are simply repeated; in other words, that we regroup around the same centre. Will Logos once again dominate and suppress Sophia?

In the midst of this re-forming of relationships – with Germany, with Russia, and with the Middle-East – questions must be asked: What is God saying to our world today? How is God speaking? What is God saying about the way religion has been used and misused to support the dominating structures of the colonialism of Europe's past? Is there a new word of revelation amid the turmoil of these events bringing about a changed consciousness? Do we hear it?

The Christian faith looks to both past and future: it is both involved with history and called to be prophetic (even if in practice it trails along in the wake of great events). Yet it is nourished by the belief that God's passionate presence in history is constant, dynamic and ever unfolding. Hence the 'kairos' of the moment will lie in discovering how God *now* is revealing new meaning and possibilities for justice, peace and integrity of creation.[7] Along with the collapse of many foundations of culture is the risk that *our understanding of revelation is inadequate to hear God's self-communication, to be aware of God's special presence to our times.* The words of the old Christmas carol 'O hush the noise, ye men of strife, and hear the angels sing',[8] may in fact be urging us to a deeper listening, to what Adrienne Rich has called a 'severer listening',[9] to the many conflicting discourses, gaps, silences and discontinuities, which may be more significant than the discourses issuing from the corridors of power.

'Revelation' has traditionally meant divinely revealed knowledge, unattainable for 'man' by 'his' own efforts. St Thomas Aquinas saw revealed truths not as in conflict with, but as complementary to natural theology. According to the latter, it is possible to come to some understanding of God by reason, through human experience of, for example, beauty in nature or human finitude. The danger of this argument has always been

11

that revealed truth could be hauled in to 'plug the gaps' of natural theology. But the problem is even more complex. If revelation means the 'unveiling of what is hidden', this is coherent if God is understood as pure Spirit, transcendent, 'dwelling in unapproachable light' in a supernatural world, separate from our universe; but if God is also immanent to the material world and to the depths of the human spirit, then the totality of human experience and perception is intimately bound up with knowledge of God.

Another difficulty is that revelation has come to be identified with revealed truths, or rational propositions, whose authority is guaranteed by an external source, either the Bible, tradition, or the teaching magisterium of the Church. But this means a focus on reasoned knowing, on rationality, which has been interpreted as opposed to feeling and emotion. 'Knowing God' – despite the passionate and erotic language of the Song of Songs and the mystics – has been much more an affair of mind than of heart or body.

Again, revelation has often been thought to consist of 'timeless truths'. Yet these truths come to us clothed in the language, concepts and world-view from which they emerged. (For example, St Thomas's famous Five Ways are dependent on the medieval philosophy of substance and Aristotle's distinction between potency and act.) What of the faith-experience of the believer today which issues from a totally different matrix of experience? What kind of formative influence should be acknowledged? Finally, who is excluded from the very proclamation of revealed truth – from its sources, its transmission and its contemporary elucidation?

Let us remember Sophia of the introductory story, excluded from the conference which was to shape Europe's future. There are three reasons why this has been the case and may remain so. First, the word in which doctrine is proclaimed too often issues from the 'high thrones of patriarchy' (the phrase is Rosemary Ruether's) without paying attention to the *consensus fidelium*, the wider experience of believers in a given context. When Word/Logos/Reason are made synonymous with 'order' and establishment, vast areas of human experience can be swept under the carpet. 'In the beginning is the relation',[10] said Martin Buber, calling our attention to the relational situation which can either evoke a response in speech or prevent it, for those who have no access to the word. Hence prior to the word must be the 'sharper listening', in order that a different discourse be heard and the 'music of Sophia', which represents the narratives of suffering and exclusion, be discerned.

Second, Christian revelation is called to respond in humility to the changed inter-faith scene. Sophia-Wisdom is by no means the prerogative of Christianity. Thus Christianity is called to a vast movement of *metanoia*, or repentance, for its failure to recognize and listen to the revealed word of other faiths and to listen with humility to other wisdoms.

Third, it must face the implications of the exclusion of women from revelation, both in the specific content of what counts as revealed truth and in the fact that women have been largely excluded from the official teaching bodies of the Church (although this now varies among the denominations). How would the content of revelation differ if the experience of women – within an exploration of all the cultural differences this implies – was a formative factor? And if women become participators in the process, will our patterns of relating with creation also be transformed?

First, the position of woman, silent outsider to official revelation, needs to be highlighted, before embarking upon the process of weaving new metaphors for revelation.

2 Woman: Silent Outsider to Revelation

The technology of silence
The rituals, etiquette

The blurring of terms
silence not absence

of words or music or even
raw sounds

Silence can be a plan
rigorously executed

the blueprint to a life

It is a presence
it has a history a form

Do not confuse it
with any kind of absence

(Adrienne Rich, 'Cartographies of Silence', in *The Dream of a Common Language*)

If we had a keen vision and feeling of all ordinary human life, it would be like hearing the grass grow, and the squirrel's heart-beat, and we should die of that roar which lies on the other side of silence. (George Eliot, *Middlemarch*)

CAN THE MARGIN BECOME THE CENTRE?

This chapter reflects on what the position of woman, as silent outsider to official revelation, has meant to the way the content of Christian faith is understood, and, more importantly, how it has affected its praxis. Has the fact of women being denied full human subjectivity by the patriarchal ordering of society – both in biblical times and sweeping through the history of Christendom – as well as having been denied access to the process of forming authoritative tradition, had a damaging effect on Christian perception of revelation and its content? The difficulty of access to 'woman's experience' and its

14

revelatory content will be explored in the following chapter.

As a haunting image of woman as outsider to revelation I use the biblical figure of Hagar, the concubine of Abraham (Gen. 16.1–16; 21.1–21).[1] Hagar is outsider in terms of race (she is Egyptian), class (she is a slave), and sex (she is a woman). What is more, she is a prototype of an oppressed woman, oppressed both by the patriarchal system as well as by another woman, Sarah, 'the patriarchal woman'. (The ambiguity of Sarah's position must not be lost sight of: although she has a limited power and status as the wife of a patriarch, yet her status as a human subject is severely limited, and is related to the task of providing an heir for Abraham. Caught within this value system she becomes an oppressor of another, less privileged woman.)

Hagar is also the prototype of a woman fleeing patriarchy to wander in the desert, since she is flung, not once but twice into the wilderness. In a sense she is the anti-type of Israel enslaved in Egypt. Here an Egyptian woman is oppressed in Israel: she is flung into the desert, without the solace of a covenant relationship, or the lure of the Promised Land. Hagar's death is not even recorded, although we hear of her son, Ishmael, again. Yet for me she is the figure of woman, bearer of revelation, but ignored by 'mainstream' tradition.

For Hagar is the first mother of a child of promise, whose birth is foretold by an angel. Alone, abandoned, she 'sees' and receives a revelation:

> And the angel of the Lord said to her, 'Behold you are with child, and shall bear a son; you shall call his name Ishmael; because the Lord has given heed to your affliction.' (Gen. 16.11)

She is astounded, not only by the news of the forthcoming baby but *because she has seen God and lived*: So she called the name of the Lord who spoke to her, 'Thou art a God of seeing'; for she said, 'Have I really seen God and remained alive after seeing him?' (Gen. 16.13)

Already Hagar acts to jolt us into a different reading of the Bible. For the Gospel of John and the First Letter of John tell us that no man has ever seen God (John 1.18; 1 John 4.12): the fact that an outcast woman is the bearer of a vision of God, knew it and survived, is not considered to be of any importance. But she speaks to us today across the centuries, as a call to repentance for the way women have treated other women, and as a summons to listen to the voice of revelation from the discourse of minorities.

It is not only as isolated individuals that women are outsiders to the tradition. American Jewish feminist scholar Judith Plaskow has constructed a new Jewish systematic theology, placing women central to Jewish tradition, instead of on the margins.[2] And why was this necessary? Because women did not stand at Sinai, as bearers of the covenant with God. She cites Moses as he prepares the people to receive the divine covenant:

> So Moses went down from the mountain to the people, and consecrated the people; and they washed their garments. And he said to the people, 'Be ready by the third day; do not go near a woman.' (Exod. 19.14–15)

In other words, women were excluded from the foundational experience for Judaism, the receiving of the revelation of the divine covenant. Jewish law did not recognize women as full human subjects. Christian revelation too sees its roots in this covenantal experience. 'The People of God' in covenantal relationship with God, wandering through the desert to the Promised Land, is an inspirational image for the Christian Church.[3] Yet women cannot look back to this image of Church as inspirational, for they are only marginal and relative within it. And thus it remains throughout Scripture. For example, when Matthew tells the story of Jesus feeding the five thousand (Matt. 14.13–21), we would assume that this figure would include men, women and children. Yet Matthew says 'And those who ate were about five thousand men, not to mention the women and the children' (Matt. 14.21).

Thus a hermeneutic of suspicion is introduced to the way we read the Bible. On how many occasions does 'people' actually mean 'men', thus reducing women and children to shadowy, marginal status? What would happen if the experience of the margins became central?

For many women today the experience of being in the 'wilderness' is the only appropriate way to describe their position. As Rosemary Ruether expressed it,

We are not in exile, but the Church is in exodus with us. God's Shekinah, Holy Wisdom, the Mother-face of God has fled from the high thrones of patriarchy and has gone into exodus with us.[4]

This was highlighted in a striking way in Britain by the Wilderness Service held outside the doors of Southwark Cathedral at the Ordination Service in 1985. At the moment of communion the women marched out of the cathedral, symbolizing that because ordination was denied to them, they were not in communion. In fact they were in the wilderness like Hagar and would remain so until admitted by the Church of England to the ordained priesthood. That is but one example; there are hundreds more. The point being made here is not simply to bemoan marginal status: it is to challenge the centre from the margins. It is also to regroup on the margins, in the discovery of new forms of community, with new meanings for ancient symbols and rituals, thus creating space for a new word to spill forth among us. It is to seek, in this desert, to break out of the aridity and abandonment of the wilderness experience through discovering, as Hagar did, small pools of water to nourish our thirst for community and justice. In so doing, the margin becomes the centre for a new process of growth. Not that this new centre of growth would re-create the unjust power patterns of the old. Rather, it is hoped that power relations will be transformed. The prevailing ethic will move from dominance to reciprocity, from hierarchical control to openness, difference, pluriformity and dialogue. Only from the margins – from the notion of power transformed by the powerless – and from the wilderness experience, can the discourse of patriarchy be unmasked and dismantled.

THE INVISIBILITY OF WOMEN WITHIN MODELS OF REVELATION

The theme of marginality and invisibility can be further highlighted by looking at the different ways in which revelation has been understood. Here I use the schema of Avery Dulles in his book *Models of Revelation*.[5] I will interweave this, where appropriate, with asking what way of knowing underlies a particular model. The question needs to be posed as to whether different epistemological categories are at work in the way in which we come to grasp how God is speaking to us. Is gender difference also a factor here? In other words, has the experience of being marginal, as well as the qualitatively different experiences of being male and female, some bearing on the way in which men and women have come to know, to be receptive to the presence and word of God?

Dulles is well aware of the tension between revelation and human experience; he is convinced of the need to take into consideration the ways in which Churches have used the concept of revelation to enhance their claims and authority, and the way in which biblical criticism, linguistic analysis, epistemological categories, the psychology of dreams, as well as philosophical agnosticism, have all challenged the supposedly 'divine-given' element of revelation in relation to so-called 'purely human experience'. But although he is also aware of the counter-claims of faiths other than Christianity, and the contribution of the empirical sciences, the total lack of gender awareness which he displays challenges the validity of these models of revelation as being of lasting significance. I will now show what this lack of gender awareness means – still as an attempt to prepare the way towards 'asking the right question' (which was the concern of chapter 1).

These models should be seen as 'strands' present in history, rather than as self-contained units or even as being mutually exclusive of each other. Thus the first model which Dulles describes is self-explanatory and most familiar, even if the most problem-fraught. That is, revelation is understood as doctrine, divinely authoritative doctrine. God is the ultimate guarantor of this doctrinal truth, whose validity and unchanging expression are safeguarded by the publicly-legitimated ecclesiastical authority.

But, without disputing the necessity of doctrinal statements, feminist theology, black theology and liberation theology from all continents are asking, If these doctrinal 'truths' have been articulated and proclaimed by those in power, what has happened to the experience of those 'on the underside of history', those who have always been denied access to the word of proclamation? Could there be a revelation, also divinely-given, which is issuing from the wilderness experience? What

18

are the images of God emerging from concrete, historical situations of marginalization? Just as Sophia challenged Logos, the challenge has to be posed to the 'word' of dogma: how does it relate to the stories and experiences of suffering? What could revelation mean to those whose life-experience has forced them into silence?

These questions must be linked with the traditional difficulty of discerning which doctrinal expressions belong to a particular culture and which might be described as the essential core of the doctrine.[6] Should we not also see this question as linked with power relations? Is it an accident that women are still regarded as unfit candidates for ordination in many churches, when the controlling positions are held by men, the prime human subject is understood as male and the redeemer necessarily male?

Dulles presents as his second model revelation as salvation history,[7] as a manifestation of God's saving power by actions within history. Here the problem is to discern *which* events are revelatory. Is the whole of history to be seen as the arena of God's saving action, or merely certain key events? Even if we adopt the perspective of liberation theologians (for example, Gutiérrez and Bonino) that revelation occurs where liberation and the achievements of human justice are incarnate in human history, we still have to ask *whose* liberation is achieved and at the expense of whom? The liberation theologians themselves admit to having been blind to the experience of women in their own contexts. James Cone, sometimes called the 'Father of black theology' writes:

> Why have black theologians been silent on this point (sexism) when we have been relentless in our critique of the racist practices of white Churches? I do not see how we can keep our credibility as 'liberation theologians' and remain so unliberated in our dealing with the question of sexism. Nearly all black theologians have either ignored sexism completely, or made such irrelevant comments on it that silence would have been preferable.[8]

Is there not something élitist and exclusivist about claiming God's revelation in such a way that the experience of divine revelation in great faiths other than Christianity is not taken seriously? The challenge of defining what is to count as 'salvation history' is then to decide what is to be excluded by

19

the particular definition chosen. Do we not then run into the danger of restricting divine revelation to certain events, which 'we' (that is, those in power positions) dignify as 'key', as the core of faith, and thus become deaf to the 'silent music' of God's ceaselessly ongoing communication?

If we recall the music of Sophia – which evoked forgotten traditions of culture and community, life-styles closely interacting with the environment, and the memories and hopes of suffering people – we are forced to ask what has happened to the unrecorded experience, the unremembered, the vast uncharted area which never came to articulation, and thus never formed part of the canon of revelation. Bringing this to articulation could challenge the emphasis we lay on certain doctrines at the expense of others, as well as offering another perspective on the periods into which we have divided our history. For example, how could the Renaissance really signify rebirth of culture if enormous groups of humanity were excluded from such a phenomenon? Or, when we speak of the Enlightenment as the crucial phenomenon of modern civilization, is this not to claim too much, when women and many so-called 'primitive' peoples were still excluded from the normative understanding of human subjectivity?[9]

Third in Dulles's classification is revelation as inner experience, as the 'self-manifestation of God in the depth of the human spirit', as the 'welling up of the Divine within'. The German philosopher Friedrich Schleiermacher, writing at the beginning of the nineteenth century, saw every communication of the universe to 'man' as revelatory. On the face of it, this way of seeing revelation seems to show promise for the lost experience of women. It has clear links with romanticism and appeals to romantic feminism which was popular in the nineteenth century.[10] I would see, for example, George Eliot's rejection of established religion and search for a wider sense of the whole as an expression of this. The sense in which Dorothea, heroine of *Middlemarch*, sought in 'the widening the skirts of light'[11] to make the divine presence more manifest, reflects this intuition of the immanent divine. However, the appeal to a supposed 'inner' experience is fraught with pitfalls.

In the first place, what is disputed is the criterion for relating the significance of the individual's inner experience to a group's communitarian experience: what status, authority and driving force should it have? (This question has become known as the validity of 'private revelation'.) It has become a tragic issue in the cases of certain individuals claiming to have a divine mission to murder women. It has been a particularly severe problem for women, the authenticity of whose visions has frequently been denied. And yet, in many cases, the relationship of the visions of these women to their Christian community has been explicit. Leaving aside the visions of Joan of Arc (problematic because of their political content), the story of Hildegarde of Bingen (1098–1179) is remarkable. Hildegarde organized her community of Benedictine sisters at Rupertsberg in the Rhineland according to the inspiration of her visions.[12] There is no suggestion of a 'private' revelation. Again, two hundred years later, the nuns of Helfta, Gertrud and Mechtild of Magdeburg, used their visions, which were eucharistic in content, to establish their authority in the Church, where the position and authority of women was being undermined.[13] So we have a paradox: the authority of womens' visions is frequently questioned (Teresa of Avila had great difficulty in being believed, for example), and yet the timing of these visions seems to have strengthened the authority of women where this was being undermined.

Second, the problem of articulating inner experience, in a manner satisfactory to both visionary and interpreting community, is often insurmountable. Classically, this is recognized to be the paradox of trying to express the inexpressible and ineffable: 'God dwells in unapproachable light', we are told by the Russian Orthodox tradition. Even if a rich enough language were to exist which could bear the weight of the divine, it would come adrift on the quicksands of the verifiability problem,[14] as philosophers of religion have been at pains to point out. Nor, as they tell us, is the notion of a self-authenticating vision a compelling one. The visionary will tend to name her experience according to images and concepts available to her from her faith tradition. The circularity of this process thus eliminates verifiability. The history of women visionaries shows this to be a complex question.

For example, the nineteenth-century visionary, Bernadette Soubirous of Lourdes in France, made no claims that the

'Lady' she saw was Mary the Mother of Jesus. When ordered to challenge the 'Lady' as to her identity, she received the answer 'I am the Immaculate Conception', a dogma of the Roman Catholic Church only recently defined in 1854. This asthmatic poor peasant child would scarcely have heard the expression and, if she had, would not have been able to understand it. The fact that Lourdes – despite the aspects of commercialization associated with it, and the political motives for the Church's encouraging of Lourdes as a pilgrimage centre – has become a place above all of prayer and healing, indicates that if a vision is 'revelatory' in an ecclesial sense, its significance extends far beyond the private experience of the individual. And yet . . . and yet. . . . Why is Bernadette remembered and, until recently, Hildegarde, with her rich theology of creation, almost totally forgotten? Does it have more to do with social and political factors than with the content of the original revelation?

We must not overlook the fact that in many cultures visions of Mary are associated with the marginalized 'little peoples' who are threatened with submersion by the dominant culture. For example, the devotion to Our Lady of Guadeloupe in Mexico originated in the apparitions of 1531, ten years after the Indian culture in Mexico was overrun by white Europeans. Here, the links with the older pagan Goddess traditions also cannot be overlooked.[15]

The struggle which women have had to gain access to the word, to articulate what must be very different experiences from what is accepted as the 'dominant' human one, and to be given credibility once these are articulated, requires urgent consideration.

Even the very division itself of 'inner' from 'outer' experience needs to be challenged: perhaps these very categories are the consequences of a dualistic world-view. Thus attention must be given to gender difference in the way human persons come to know. The question is now raised as to whether womens' different experience regarding access to knowledge and education calls for new epistemological categories. This is explored by the authors of *Women's Ways of Knowing*,[16] in a way helpful for a new understanding of revelation. The writers, as a result of their research among academic women from nine different institutions and women involved in 'family agencies', suggest five ways of knowing. The first is 'silence'. It is indeed the very silence on which this chapter is focusing – the absence of women from official tradition and doctrine – but concretizes this in a significant way. For the women represented here do not have any 'inner experience'. They cannot articulate their feelings, or what they know, because their life-experience has eliminated all basic self-confidence. Experience of violence has often removed ability to protest. They remain passive, subdued, with little or no self-esteem. They have no possibility of making sense of their own experiences and often assume they are to blame for their own situation. Scripturally speaking, their situation is epitomized by the terrible story of the concubine in Judges 19.

While her master is entertained by an old man at Gibeah, the concubine (and the man's young daughter) were given to the men of the town:

> And they knew her, and abused her all night until the morning. And as dawn began to break, they let her go. And as morning appeared, the woman came and fell down at the door of the man's house where her master was, till it was light.
> And her master rose up in the morning, and . . . behold, there was his concubine lying at the door of the house, with her hands on the threshold. He said, 'Get up, let us be going'. But there was no answer. (Judg. 19.25–8)[17]

In fact, she never speaks again, rendered voiceless by her brutal violation. In what must be the most horrific Bible story revealing contempt for women, we are shown how revenge against the Benjaminites for the crime was sought by killing the woman, and dividing her body into twelve parts as a means of summoning the twelve tribes of Israel to revenge. In other words, the crime was that the man's property had been misused, not that a woman had been abused. The silence which cries out from this story is that nowhere does the Bible condemn this explicitly as a crime against female sexuality.

The second 'way of knowing' which the authors offer is that of 'received knowledge'.[18] This is listening to the voices of others. But it is not the creative way of listening for which I have been calling. It is a belief that knowledge is acquired by

23

listening to authorities; learning is identified with receiving and repeating the words of authorities. Thus womens' own voices are never to be trusted. Women remain passive and dependent knowers. Unfortunately, if we now recall that a dominant model of revelation has been 'receiving' divinely-authorized doctrine in the form of propositions and technical statements, for example, incarnation as 'hypostatic union of divine–human natures' (Dulles' Model 1), it is clear that not only women, but anyone taught in this fashion, will neither discover their own voice nor achieve integration of head and heart. Sadly, the contemporary education system is still permeated with 'received knowers', mechanically handing on what they themselves have received as unchangeable truth. Learning becomes the memorizing and reproduction of authorized words. Knowledge is always from the top downwards, never in the other direction.

The third 'way of knowing' is subjective knowing.[19] Its relevance for the models of revelation under discussion lies in its focus on the emergence of the subjective voice (truth as intuited within personal experience). It is the mode of knowing underlying revelation as inner experience. What is interesting from the examples given is that the subjective voices emerge as a result of *failed male authority*. For example, a Catholic woman who returned to study because she needed to develop her skills and support her children, found support from a womens' discussion group:

> I always thought there were rules and that if you followed the rules, you'd be happy. And I never understood why I wasn't. I'd get to thinking . . . I'm good, I follow the rules. I do everything they tell me to, and things don't go right for me. My life was a mess. I wrote to a priest that I was very fond of and I asked him, 'What do I do to make things right?' He had no answers. This time it dawned on me that I was not going to get the answers from anybody. I would have to find them myself.[20]

The importance of the 'subjective voice' can hardly be overestimated. I have already referred to its importance as source of authority, for example, in the visions of the nuns of Magdeburg. But the difficulty it presents as a way of understanding divine revelation, is not simply the problem of

24

articulation of 'inner' experience. It is that women who remain operating at the level of 'gut feeling', or intuition, may very well have important insights. But they frequently lack the ability to integrate these within a total world-view. When confronted with a conflicting theory, or point of view, they are helpless, as they lack the tools – or theory of knowledge – which could bring them to a wider understanding. Intuitive, subjective knowing is often accompanied by a rejection of received knowing (in the form of 'the tradition') by a crude fundamentalism, by pragmatism (what is true is what works best for me), and by alienation from all things scientific. It can be most damaging to women who for the first time are trying to be recognized as culture-builders and as having played an active part in history.

There is an even deeper problem to be faced. Is it not possible that this split between inner experience and its articulation in a wider community is the product of the subject/object split, where the human subject is seen as sharply divided from the surrounding world, which is viewed as object? If this is so, then the modern predicament which has been proclaimed for the last thirty years as one of alienation and estrangement,[21] from ourselves, each other and the environment, admits of a different explanation. While it may be true that we are 'out of tune' with nature, that

getting and spending we lay waste our powers,
(Wordsworth)[22]

could it not be that this alienation is consequent on our way of viewing the world and God, and that from the discourses on the margins is springing another way of viewing humanity's relation to the wider world?

The current philosophical wisdom is proclaiming that our modern culture has broken up: post-modernism announces that we have no metaphor to describe ourselves, no over-arching paradigm to describe our age's fragmentation. We are, said the American theologian David Tracy, with great melancholy, the age without a name.[23] Yet modernism has scarcely permitted the full subjectivity of women – so its fragmentation is scarcely such a tragedy!

The hope of this book is to explore the possibility of a

connected vision based on a connected way of knowing. (This is the fifth model from *Women's Ways of Knowing*, and will be explored later in chapters 4 and 5.) This, despite its submerged and marginal status, has not yet been totally destroyed. But can it be brought from the margin to the centre in time to halt the furious journey to destruction which seems to be our civilization's course? And when brought to light, will 'connectedness' have the articulacy and expressive power to cut through the inner/outer tensions which have haunted this third model of revelation under discussion?

To return to Dulles's *Models of Revelation*, the fourth model or strand of traditional revelation categories can be described as *dialectical presence*. This refers to God's address to those whom 'He' encounters with word in Scripture and Christian proclamation. It was an important model for Martin Luther as well as for Rudolph Bultmann. The latter saw the stress on the kerygma as the source of revelatory encounter. Proclaiming the word has again assumed fundamental significance for us in contemporary times, with the announcing of a decade devoted to evangelism. Proclamation of the revelatory word is indeed rooted in Jesus' own proclamation that the Kingdom of God was at hand (Mark 1.15), and in Christianity's conviction that Jesus himself was the self-communicating Word of God, the Word abiding in the heart of God from all eternity and made flesh in Jesus of Nazareth.

Where, then, lies the problem? Although Christian tradition has been aware of the need for doctrine to develop and the tension (already referred to) between the supposed core of truth which the doctrine contains and its 'outer' cloak of culturally-rooted images, concepts and formulations, it has seldom reflected on the *sociological status of 'Word' as such and its connection with power and status.* The question is, who proclaims the word and who decides on its content? At the end of the twentieth century we can no longer afford to be so innocent about the limits of language: as Adrienne Rich writes,

> There are words I cannot choose again:
> *humanism androgyny*
>
> Such words have no shame in them, no diffidence
> before the raging stoic grandmothers:

their glint is too shallow, like a dye
that does not permeate

the fibers of actual life
as we live it now.[24]

Can we ever be innocent of grammar and washed free of the
guilt of words? That is an acute question in an age which
believes in being 'economical with the truth';[25] an age in which
an American president can refer to the atom bomb as 'God's
little peace-maker'; when killing Iraqi soldiers is disguised by
referring to the 'degradation' of the army. This new awareness
of 'the guilt of words' takes on fresh significance when linked
with *Women's Ways of Knowing*'s fourth model, *procedural
knowledge*.[26] Viewed positively, procedural knowledge is a
valuable tool. Through it students are given structures and
procedures for arguments, criticism and evaluation. It offers a
way forward from subjectivism and 'gut feeling', and avoids a
crude fall-back into fundamentalism, a shrill insistence on
one's own feelings, or resentment towards authority without
the means of articulation. Its drawback is that a kind of
intellectual exultance in the power of the argument can lead to
indifference to the outcome of the process. 'It doesn't matter
what I decide as long as the steps of the argument are correct' is
sometimes heard as justification of this line of approach. This
encourages emotional detachment from the process and a
dangerous objectivity. It is encountered in theology where
reason and religious experience are sharply separated from
each other, and where theological argument is not recognized
as issuing from a particular cultural context.

Whereas we need not take the 'cultured' despair of post-
modernism too seriously, its critique that culture is not a
seamless garment should certainly be heeded. If we are in fact a
civilization of many overlapping discourses, then 'the word'
invites different cultural interpretations. For example, the
concepts of 'freedom' and 'liberation' before, during and after
communism and capitalism still struggle for 'authentic'
interpretation and realization.

Thus the key question now is, whether we are prepared to
give attention to the silences, gaps, discontinuities in the
proclamation of the Word. Are we prepared to ask awkward

27

questions as to whose voice is excluded from official discourse? We would hope then for a Church able to respond in terms of a *listening metanoia*, a developing consciousness of the link between word and power. If the marginal discourse was encouraged to burst into speech, if we became aware of the Mother-face of God in Exodus and exile, could this bring about the dismantling of patriarchy? Yes, revelation as word and proclamation – but only if we listen to the discourses of the marginalized.

Dulles's fifth model is that of 'new awareness'. This model – which offers much promise to feminist theology, indeed to all liberation theologies – sees revelation as the dawning of a different consciousness, as a call to fuller participation in the divine work of creating and redeeming. It arises out of the inadequacy of previous models and sees God's speaking to us as a call to new awareness, a call which forms a crucial part of this conscious-raising process. The question will be, What is the content of this new awareness?

Making use of this model, aware of the absence of women in revelatory paradigms, in doctrine, history and proclamation of the word, feminist theology calls attention to womens' part as recipients of divine revelation and proclaimers of the word. Mary's fiat, 'Be it done unto me according to your Word' (Luke 1.38) becomes understood not as passive acquiescence but active response to the energizing presence of God. Even though much attention is now given to revelation not merely as 'propositional' but as God's communication through myth, parable, poem and dream, we have never been told that the dreams of women could be revelatory. When Joseph of Nazareth had a dream, 'Joseph son of David, do not fear to take Mary your wife . . .' (Matt. 1.20), we are not told what Mary dreamt. In fact there is but one reported woman's dream in the Bible, that of Calpurnia, wife of Pontius Pilate: 'Have nothing to do with that righteous man, for I have suffered much over him today in a dream' (Matt. 27.19). A Roman woman perceives a Jewish man to be righteous, but her husband washes his hands of the affair.

Today this is being remedied by the emphasis of feminist writers, such as Carol Christ and Naomi Goldenberg, on the importance of attending to dreams for womens' social and spiritual quest, and for the process of psychic transformation. But the question of how to interpret dreams and visions as sources of revelation for the Christian community brings the next question to the fore: How do we get in touch with 'authentic experience' which is only accessible through the dominant interpreting discourses? Anything notionally authentic is necessarily perceived through these filters. Chapter 3 focuses on this question.

3 Living the Sacrifice and the Lost Experience of Women

SONIA AND THE SACRIFICE OF FEMALE SUBJECTIVITY

The time is the nineteenth century, and the story unfolds in a sparse garret in St Petersburg, by the dim light of a candle. A thin, pale-faced girl with brilliant eyes, 'blue and soft but which could yet dart such lights', is reading aloud in a trembling voice the story, from the Gospel of John, of Jesus raising Lazarus to life, Jesus who is thus revealed as 'the resurrection and the life'. The story is revelatory in a double sense. First, it is the *evangelist's* way of revealing Jesus' power over life and death; second, it is the *novelist's* way of depicting the power of revelation to transform the life of a man. It will now be evident that the girl is Sonia, a prostitute, the man Raskolnikoff, a murderer; the novel is Dostoevsky's *Crime and Punishment*. Its significance here is as an encounter with divine revelation:

> The dying piece of candle dimly lit up this low-ceilinged room, in which an assassin and a harlot had just read the Book of Books.[1]

Already the role of Sonia in this great story of redemption has been made clear to the reader. Raskolnikoff has interrogated her as to why she leads this debased and shocking life. Dostoevsky leaves us under no illusion about the nature of the self-sacrifice which Sonia has made. She has absolutely no alternative if her family is to be saved from starvation; she is aware that she faces a horrible death, possibly in public. Raskolnikoff jumps up and bows to her: 'I did not bow to you personally, but to suffering humanity in your person'.

For Dostoevsky, Sonia is a figure of Christ, the Suffering Servant and redemptive mediator. As such, there is no question of justice for Sonia herself. She is the sacrificial means of bringing the murderer to repentance. As the reading progresses, its immense emotional impact as revelation for Sonia heightens:

She was getting to the miraculous story, and a feeling of triumph was taking possession of her. Her voice, strengthened by joy, had a metallic ring. The lines became misty to her troubled eyes, but, fortunately, she knew the passage by heart.

When it comes to the words, 'I am the Resurrection and the Life; he that believeth in me, tho' he were dead, yet shall he live', she has difficulty in breathing. It is as if

In reading the words of Martha, she was making her own Confession of faith: 'Yea, Lord, I believe that thou art the Christ, the Son of God, which should come into the world.'

Sonia's purpose in reading coincides with the central aim of John's Gospel, that the man who is morally blind – in this case Raskolnikoff – should be led to faith. It is Sonia, in the paradoxical position as utterly despicable and yet a saviour figure, who eventually brings Raskolnikoff to the point of confession: 'Sonia, I have come to carry the Cross'. It is Sonia who follows him to Siberia. At the end of the story a new life dawns for Raskolnikoff, again mediated by Sonia: 'The heart of one held within it an eternal store of light and love for the heart of the other.' The same copy of the New Testament is with them in Siberia and is again approached, this time by one who is prepared to suffer and be regenerated.

This story illustrates in two ways the difficulty of approaching the experience of women as 'raw stuff' for revelation. Not only is the experience of women invisible to the text, or suppressed from it – as was the case with the concubine of Judges 19 – but *its presence within the text is in a mediated form*. In fact, women's presence within the great Western classics is frequently in the form of mediated or *sacrificed subjectivity*. (Even women novelists have great difficulty in breaking out of the mould of doomed female subjectivity and offering to their heroines the degree of liberation which they themselves enjoyed.)[2]

It is not that Dostoevsky is to be criticized for paying scant attention to the socio-economic situation of Sonia. For the regeneration of Raskolnikoff is a spiritual one. The end of the story dramatizes this by depicting the black points of the tents of the nomads in the distance:

31

There was liberty, and other people not resembling here; there
time itself had stood still, and had not moved since the days of
Abraham and his flocks.

The scene is both biblical and archetypal. In contrast to this
vast vista of freedom, Raskolnikoff is in prison. But the
spiritual dawn of resurrection will transcend this.

Thus Dostoevsky is not directly addressing the cruelty of
the system he lives in, in a story which primarily focuses on
moral regeneration. (He has made it clear that he had many
good reasons to criticize the system.) Nor should the theme of
self-renunciation itself be criticized. It is the use which the
writer makes of the theme which is the problem. Dostoevsky
has no interest in Sonia herself except as mediator. Her
mediated subjectivity means that the power of the gospel as
revelation cannot change *her* situation in the way that Jesus'
encounter with the woman in adultery changed hers (John 7).
For Sonia, in Dostoevsky's eyes, dying to self meant totally
giving up on this life in the service of the redemption of
another. No attention at all is devoted to her loss of self-worth,
her wronged sexuality. Sonia's love for Raskolnikoff is
depicted as true Christian agape (self-giving love) in its
classical interpretation, as opposed to eros (love seeking its own
satisfaction). In idealizing the paradoxical role of the prostitute-
redemptress Dostoevsky conceals the fact of her sacrificed,
mediated subjectivity. It is the significance of 'living the
sacrifice' of mediated subjectivity which I now explore in
order to understand what potential the hidden experience of
women may have for revelation.

MOTHERHOOD AS REMEDY FOR HAVING BEEN BORN AS WOMAN? *AND YOU SHALL BE SAVED THROUGH BEARING CHILDREN.*

The theme of the lost or the mediated subjectivity of women is
clearest when we look at motherhood as the socially-approved
way of being woman.[3] I will explore this with an example from
the Christian scriptures (1 Tim. 2.11–15) and through the
work of Julia Kristeva, Professor of Linguistics, philosopher
and psychoanalyst. The central question will be: If motherhood
has been the way in which female subjectivity has been
traditionally lived out – both in biological motherhood and in

'motherly roles' such as nursing, teaching and social work – is there a language of the self for women once this discourse has been challenged, as indeed it now has?

If we look at the question theologically, it becomes evident that motherhood has been associated intrinsically with re-demption for women. Indeed it has been extolled as the only means of salvation and linked with the supposed extra responsibility which women carry for the fall. As Luise Schotroff, a German feminist theologian, writes in her *Letter to Adam*:

> Paul said that through you sin came into the world. But Christian men have maintained all through the centuries that it was Eve's fault. . . . Already in the First Letter to Timothy your friends began the campaign against Eve: 'Let a woman learn in silence and all submissiveness. I permit no woman to teach or have authority over men; she is to keep silent. For Adam was formed first and then Eve; and Adam was not deceived, but the woman was deceived and became a transgressor. Yet woman will be saved through bearing children . . .' (1 Tim.2.11–15 RSV) Later the Christian men said it more clearly: Eve slept with the snake and thereby brought sin into the world.[4]

The citation from 1 Timothy spells out dramatically what is often implicit: not only that motherhood is the intrinsically 'natural' role for women, but that it is the only means of atonement for belonging to the same sex as Eve. Christianity has explicitly taught that in motherhood is both the glory and pain of being woman. The icon of Mary, Virgin-Mother, is held before us – particularly in the Catholic tradition – as the epitome of womanhood.

At the end of the twentieth century a particularly severe crisis has been reached. In certain parts of the world economic advances, better health and educational opportunities have made a range of options possible for women, where motherhood may be valued less by many women than a chosen career. Advances in reproductive technology – *in vitro* fertilization and surrogate motherhood – have meant that a range of choices has become available to parenting, involving a new range of ethical decisions. For many women, friendship, and woman-identified friendship at that, is what gives deep significance and happiness to their lives.[5]

Despite this degree of freedom, or perhaps because of it, the incidence of violence against women *within* marriage has increased (and this is to focus on one area alone). Being a mother may entrap a woman into accepting a level of violence for the sake of children or to preserve the peace. Looking to the poorer parts of the world it is women as mothers who are witnesses to the deepest suffering of the world. Mercy Amba Oduyoye, a Ghanaian theologian, writes in 'Motherhood and Poverty':

> The impoverishment of women in Africa is an aspect of the impoverishment of the Third World which had remained undisclosed or ignored until women themselves made their voices heard. Whatever poverty women as mothers struggle with cannot be understood apart from the real poverty-maker, power, the inability to influence decisions that condition one's life.[6]

I saw a painful illustration of her words in a visit with my husband to drought-stricken areas of Rajasthan in northern India. As the village wells dried up, the women and young girls were forced to walk further and further several times a day in the heat to collect water. Yet they were not part of the decision-making processes of the village. When an attempt was made to involve them in the discussions, the response was 'water is not a womens' issue'!

Although feminist thought has been productive for the past twenty years in publicizing the extent to which motherhood has been the subject of social and economic control, and in balancing the gains which new techniques have brought against accompanying medicalization and high technological dependency,[7] the extent to which motherhood is still subject to theological and ecclesial control has not been elucidated. Motherhood is still depicted in Church documents as being essentially *the same* throughout history. Also the way in which mothers are used to nurture the kind of individual desired by the state has not been made clear. *Women have been colonized by individualism*, says Elizabeth Fox-Genovese; motherhood itself is the very vehicle of individualism.[8] The challenge still has to be faced: if the experience of women is a priori the experience of motherhood, spiritual or biological, and if this discourse is rejected, does Christian theology have any alternative discourse for women?

34

To show that motherhood is still the official ecclesial discourse for women I have to show how the ghost of 1 Timothy is still with us. Even though the intention of the second-century writer was probably to affirm the value of having children, in the teeth of a second-century spirituality stressing flight from the world and the excesses of Gnosticism, the text has been given three sorts of interpretations which have had an impact on the lives of women. The first follows the fifth-century Bishop of Constantinople, John Chrysostom, in finding the message difficult (!) and changing the meaning to the 'rearing of children' instead of simply 'having children'.[9] The salvation of women lies in the nurture of children in the broadest possible sense. Second, the interpretation of Calvin has had enormous influence. Linking women with guilt for sin, he says:

> God is better pleased with a woman who considers the conditions God has assigned her to as a calling, and submits to it, not refusing to bear the distaste of food, the illness, the difficulty, or rather the fearful anguish associated with childbirth or anything else that is her duty . . .
> In the punishment itself are the means of securing salvation.[10]

Possibly the most chilling example of this kind of interpretation is found already in the writing of the fifth-century Father, Jerome (*Against Jovinian*), in a passage extolling virginity over marriage:

> The woman will be saved if she bear children who will remain virgins: if what she has herself lost, she attains in her children, and makes up for the loss and decay of the root by the excellence of the flower and fruit.[11]

Is it any wonder, with these kinds of distortions of female sexuality, that in the nineteenth century, when anaesthesia was introduced in childbirth, there was opposition from the clergy who claimed, as Mary Daly quoting Adrienne Rich pointed out, that it would 'rob God of the deep earnest cries which arise in time and that 'The lifting of Eve's curse seemed to threaten the foundations of patriarchal religion; the cries of women in childbirth were for the glory of God the Father.'[12]

The nineteenth-century commentators were particularly fond of the text from 1 Timothy because it could give expression to the split between the public world (masculine) and the private world, over which the 'feminine' fitly reigns. For example, a British commentator Albert Barnes, in 1832, emphasizes woman's moral weakness and stresses 'The woman should remember that sin began with her'. He then allows that

> woman shall be saved from the art of impostors and from the luxury and vice of the age . . . if . . . she remains at home, cultivates modesty, and is subject to her husband and engages carefully in the training of her children.[13]

Yet woman is comforted in her guilt: though she must suffer, she is not excluded from heaven. Nor is this type of interpretation confined to the previous century. William Barclay's commentary (1956), which has had enormous impact in Britain, links motherhood-as-salvific with 'woman's place is in the home', displaying an unbelievable unconcern for what the circumstances of home might be: 'Women will find salvation, not in addressing meetings, but in motherhood, which is their crown. Whatever else is true, a woman is queen within her home.'[14]

A third type of interpretation links childbearing with the motherhood of Mary, Mother of Jesus. Commentators presumed that because one mother bore the messiah, this would be a sustaining fact for all mothers and all women. Others declared that the great childbearing of Mary has undone the work of Eve.[15] The idealizing of the motherhood of Mary as archetypal of the role of all women still holds a strong place in Christian theology and can be seen in the Apostolic Letter of Pope John Paul II, *Mulieris Dignitatem*. Despite the reflections on the mutuality between man and woman, and the significant role which women play in the Gospels, the document still manifests a lingering essentialism in its remarks about motherhood. For, according to *Mulieris Dignitatem*, Mary as Theotokos (Godbearer) signifies the fullness of perfection of 'what is characteristic of women' and of 'what is feminine',[16] specifically dwelling on 1 Tim. 2.13–14, in the context of the Eve–Mary contrast. The Letter follows an Augustinian interpretation of the fall: the domination of man over woman is the punishment for sin and is seen in the discrimination of unjust social conditions.

The notion that motherhood is what is most characteristic of woman is then further deepened: 'In this openness, in conceiving and giving birth to a child, the woman *discovers herself through a sincere gift of herself*' (italics in original).[17]

This is woman's way of participating in the creative mystery of God. It is where there is an unwarranted leap from this biological openness to creation, to an essentialist explanation of woman, that the danger becomes clear:

> At the same time this also corresponds to the psychophysiological interpretation of women and of motherhood . . . Motherhood as a human fact and phenomenon, is fully explained on the basis of the truth about the person. *Motherhood is linked to the personal structure of the woman, and to the personal dimension of the gift* (my italics).[18]

Mary's readiness at the annunciation symbolizes every woman's openness to this gift of life. The Letter explicitly connects the woman of 1 Timothy with the motherhood of Mary, through which God began a new covenant with humanity:

> Each and every time that motherhood is repeated in human history, it is always related to the covenant that God established with the human race, through the motherhood of the mother of God.[19]

The Letter's essentialist understanding of 'masculine' and 'feminine' is not my point here – and has been discussed elsewhere. Nor is this an argument to undermine the importance for us today of motherhood, parenting and caring. Quite the reverse. Here the purpose is to explore the point of intersection between motherhood, the Christian discourse of the motherhood of Mary, and what has been permitted as a discourse for women's experience. This I do through the work of Julia Kristeva.

JULIA KRISTEVA AND 'LIVING THE SACRIFICE'. IS THERE ANOTHER DISCOURSE FOR WOMEN'S EXPERIENCE?

Julia Kristeva, of Bulgarian origin and a former Marxist intellectual of the Left Bank, has been Professor of Linguistics in Paris since 1974. Not only has she profoundly influenced the world of linguistics with her view of language as a signifying process, and her emphasis on the centrality of truth and ethics for the study of language; she is also a practising psychoanalyst, and her writings embrace art history, philosophy, theology and ethics. But why is she so significant for a book on revelation? Nowhere else in contemporary writing have I found the dilemma of the subjectivity of women with regard to the social contract delineated so sharply. For Kristeva's account of the socio-symbolic contract shows the inevitability of the exclusion of women from its dominant structures and the rejection of the distinct meaning of female sexuality.

I shall explore here Kristeva's view of *the founding social contract as sacrificial for women*. It is this notion – that the social contract is founded necessarily on the separation of the child from the body of the 'archaic' mother – which forced Kristeva at one stage of her thought to dismiss religion as 'paternalistic monotheism'.[20] She then proposed an alternative ethics based on creativity and poetic language.

'Living the sacrifice' as the only permitted discourse for women as mothers is illustrated first through Kristeva's linguistic theory. She distinguishes between two dimensions, which she refers to as the *semiotic* and the *symbolic* dimensions. For her, the symbolic structure of language (as well as the way symbols are used in society) necessarily excludes the maternal and instinctual dimension of experience. For this realm of the instinctual and maternal she coins the phrase *the semiotic chora*. The chora – a word which she takes from Plato's dialogue *Timaeus* – means 'enclosed space' or 'womb'. This is constituted by drives, energy charges and basic pulsions, which in psychoanalytic terms denote the 'pre-oedipal primary processes'. The world of the semiotic chora points to what is fluid, unnameable, archaic, maternal and instinctual. Here we can regard it as a symbol for the whole realm of the instinctual. It includes both extremes: the opposite poles of life and death, of expulsion and introjection. It is also heterogeneous: it antedates the distinction between masculine and feminine. The chora gathers up these instinctual flows or pulsions, which precede all articulation, naming and socially ordering. These energy drives, says Kristeva, link the human person to the 'pre-oedipal archaic mother's body'. But this pre-oedipal mother is not to be identified with the child's actual mother, for she is anterior to the split between masculinity and feminity. The pre-oedipal mother's body is really a source for mediating the symbolic. She is a symbol which becomes the organizing principle of social relations and the instinctual drives of the semiotic chora.[21]

Here the notion of the symbolic contract is introduced for the first time. For the child cannot remain forever linked with the body of the archaic mother, that is, the world of instinct and archaic feeling. The child needs to become a speaking subject with a place in the social order: thus s/he must separate from the semiotic chora. According to Lacanian theory – on which Kristeva relies – the young child's achievement of individuation is at the cost of the loss of *jouissance*, the instinctual, fluid, joyous expression of female sexuality. Why should this be so? It follows from Kristeva's version of the symbolic social contract.

Kristeva sees the symbolic order of verbal communication and patterned order as based on *time*.[22] This is the point of reference which locates me in the symbolic order, with a before and an after. The father, as supreme guarantor of the social contract, governs the order of sign and time. Thus women, who are governed less by linear than by cyclic time, are forced into being the 'silent other' of the social contract.

This is the sacrifice which motherhood demands of women, namely, 'Become anonymous in order to pass on the social norm'. Thus in both Judaism and Christianity – as well as in Hinduism and Islam – women have been the property of their husband, sacrificing name, freedom and family ties in order to procreate the race. This pattern still repeats itself in most cultures. In present day Jordan, for example, among the Circassian race, a girl who marries may not speak or communicate with her own family for a year after the marriage, in fact until she has produced an heir. Before the birth of the baby she lives in solitude in the household of her husband. She may not speak to her parents-in-law, and becomes recognized by them only after the birth of her child.[23]

Kristeva argues that God created the world through separation, dividing light from day, man from woman and so on. Long before the coming of the Jewish people to the Promised Land, the northern semitic people worshipped maternal divinities. So, when monotheism was established as a principle of a symbolic, paternal community, not only was paganism suppressed, but also 'the greater part of agrarian civilisations, and their ideologies, women and mothers'.[24] It was necessary to maintain the separation of the sexes because, in the realm of the symbolic, for society to guarantee order, law, unity, uniquely symbolized by the transcendent God the Father, the One, this entailed the exclusion of the 'polymorphic, orgasmic body, desiring and laughing of the other sex'.[25]

For me this recalls the incident of the three angels announcing the birth of Isaac to Sarah. *And Sarah laughed* (Gen. 18.12)! Could there be an echo here of female *jouissance*, not completely extinguished by patriarchal demands?[26] Yet the patriarchal women of the Bible generally demonstrate the force of Kristeva's argument, that their place within the social contract is guaranteed by the patriarchal need to propagate the species. Their value in society, the honour accorded women, is calculated on this one function. Barrenness was thus social disgrace and, ultimately, anonymity.

In a third type of approach Kristeva develops the idea of sacrifice, through the treatment given to female sexuality within monotheism. She relates this first to incest taboo. Through this prohibition, she claims, society avoids coming face-to-face with the unnameable, the *jouissance*, or pleasure of female sexuality, which must be prohibited from the social order. (A horrifying example of this is the issue of female circumcision, still practised in Kenya and many other places. When the late President Kenyatta came to power and was asked to prohibit this, he refused to do so, on the grounds that it was a powerful social symbol. Surely this is an excruciating example of the sacrifice of becoming anonymous to pass on the social norm?) The biblical texts are seen by Kristeva as successful in showing how maternal power is subordinated to the social order which regulates social performance: this is the fulfilling of divine law in the Temple.

The relation of taboo to sacrifice is also important. Taboos are meant to forestall the need for sacrifice; the function of sacrifice is to restore the order which has been disturbed. So how does this affect women, who are already living the sacrifice of exclusion from the social order? According to Kristeva, circumcision of the son stands in place of sacrifice as a sign of alliance with the father. (For example, Abraham was not required to sacrifice his son Isaac.) The identity of the subject with 'his' God appears to be based on the separation of son from mother. It is fascinating to note the attention given by biblical scholars to the near-sacrifice of Isaac. The tension in the story mounts until the reprieve is given at the last moment.[27] Yet so such attention is given to the sacrifice of Jethro's young daughter (Judg. 11.29–40). She must die to fulfil her father's promise. As Phyllis Trible writes:

> Hers is a premeditated death, a sentence of murder passed upon an innocent victim because of the faithless vow uttered by her foolish father. These conditions shroud the request she makes of him: 'That I may go and wander upon the hills and lament my virginity'.[28]

Tragically, patriarchal memory obliterated this sacrifice and remembered the rescue of Isaac. (One can also compare the sacrifice of Iphigeneia, daughter of King Agamemnon, in order to obtain winds for the fleet to sail to Troy). There is no lament for Jethro's daughter. Yet Jethro himself becomes elevated to the ranks of the men of faith enumerated by the Epistle to the Hebrews: he is one who 'through faith conquered kingdoms, enforced justice, . . . escaped the edge of the sword, won strength out of weakness, became mighty in war, put foreign armies to flight' (Heb. 11.32–4).

In Christianity we note a development in the understanding of taboo and sacrifice in which defilement becomes interiorized. It blends with guilt and sin and becomes a new category, with the need for forgiveness, for confession through the word, all of which give a new expression for *jouissance*. Kristeva thinks here of the story of Luke 7 where a woman anoints Jesus' feet with her tears, and wipes them with her hair. Tears will become a privileged expression of *jouissance* which we see illustrated above all in the Mater Dolorosa symbolism, the weeping Madonna.

The supreme expression of sacrifice in Christianity is the love or agape of the Father, displayed in the sacrifice of the

Son. Love, says Kristeva, is immersion and identification. But there can be no identification without the death of the beloved object. Kristeva sees this symbolized in two ways in Christianity: through the Eucharist, which is a ritual of identification-in-love with the dead Christ; and through the image of the Sorrowing Mother, who cradles the dead Christ, sacrifice of love-unto-death. Yet through her tears she gives promise of resurrection. Similarly, Christian monotheism overcomes its own fears of death through the declaration of her assumption into heaven. Through the discourse of Mater Dolorosa, the motherhood of Mary gives expression to female *jouissance*.

But why should this expression be harmful to women? Kristeva's argument is, first, that because Mary conceives God without a man – and is subject to this God – an example is created which is impossible for ordinary women to follow. Second, Mary becomes Queen of Heaven and Mother of the Church, yet kneels before a child. Third, Mary gives the comforting illusion that she overcomes time and death – which we have seen to be the lynch-pin of the social contract – through the doctrine of her assumption. Finally, she repudiates ordinary women by becoming the one, unique woman, and by attaining this uniqueness through an exaggerated masochism. Here Kristeva uses the statement of Simeon, 'And a sword will pierce through your own soul' (Luke 2.35), to indicate that affliction defines the vocation of Mary, whereas the sexuality of ordinary women merits no attention.

The effects of this can be seen both in Christianity and in secular society. First, Christianity has allowed women the choice of virginity (consecrated celibacy), or of atoning for their 'carnal *jouissance*' through martyrdom (living the sacrifice through motherhood?). Here Kristeva cites the fourth-century asceticism which intertwined sexuality with death:

> For where there is death, there is also sexual copulation, and where there is no death, there is no sexual copulation either. (John Chrysostom, *On Virginity*)[29]

But in the communication of the Word women participate not so much by giving birth, but by preparing their children for baptism. (I am reminded of Mary Daly's cry, 'We have been robbed of our birthing energies!')[30]

Second, society has traditionally offered young girls two choices: identify with mother, thus sticking fast at an earlier phase of development; or raise yourself to the symbolic status of father – 'Become Daddy's girl!' – and thus rejecting your mother. Kristeva gives the tragic example of Electra of Greek mythology. Electra was incensed by Clytemnestra's affair with Aegisthus, that is, her expression of active sexuality. So Electra incited her brother Orestes to the murder of their mother, and is thus the true daughter of the symbolic father. Kristeva sees her action as sinister in the hatred of her mother's *jouissance*, her joyous sexuality: '"Let jouissance be forbidden to the mother": this is the demand of the father's daughter.'[31]

Christianity did offer female *jouissance* a limited expression through the discourse of the 'virginal-maternal', in the tears and milk of the Madonna. Think of the Byzantine icons, the medieval pictures, the hymns, prayers and devotions where this is expressed. Yet Kristeva believes this, at root, to be an expression of idealized primary narcissism, nostalgia for the lost archaic mother. She cites the ecstasies of the twelfth-century Bernard of Clairvaux who, as the Father's virginal spouse, in his visions even received drops of virginal milk. In a secular, post-modern age, the discourse of the Virgin-Mother has lost its relevance and therefore, Kristeva concludes, motherhood is without a discourse. So she calls for a new ethic, a her-ethic of the second sex. Her own solution is to reject the logic of sacrifice and separation of the social contract, but without rejecting the social contract itself, as does separatist feminism. Instead, let there be an attempt 'To find a specific discourse closer to the body and to the emotions, to the unnameable repressed by the social contract'.[32] This means recognizing the violence which the sacrifice imposed by the social contract has brought about. Literally violence against women, but also the violence of suppressed subjectivity and *jouissance*. The discourse which Kristeva calls for would lift the weight of the sacrificial and nourish society with a free and flexible discourse. It would be found most of all in the life of the creative and the imaginary. Truth is only to be found, she concludes,

> By listening, by recognizing the unspoken in all discourse, however revolutionary, by emphasizing at each point whatever

remains unsatisfied, repressed, new, eccentric, incomprehensible, that which destroys the mutual understanding of established power.[33]

Does Kristeva's suggestion offer a way forward? Could the rejection of the logic of sacrifice, and the seeking out of what has been excluded, be the key to the discovery of the lost experience? When Perceval rejected the female world of his mother Herzeloide, to attain recognition within the symbolic contract – in his case, the warrior culture – there was no clue given by the story as to what was rejected. Kristeva's psychoanalytic analysis, coupled with her understanding of how sacrifice has functioned to suppress female sexuality, has opened the door to the content of what has been excluded.

With Kristeva I seek a new discourse for women which includes, but is wider than, motherhood, but I seek its articulation within the vision of Christian feminism. I seek this discourse *within* the search for a language for women's experience. I do not seek to locate womens' experience solely within the discourse of the maternal. Womens' experience is so rich and diverse that it cannot be subsumed under this one heading. (In the following chapter I will suggest a metaphor for this experience which offers a new understanding for revelation.) Restricting womens' discourse to that of being childbearers (as we saw earlier in this chapter with the citation from 1 Timothy and its influence on *Mulieris Dignitatem*) hinders their recognition as friends, sisters, mystics, lovers, culture-bearers and traditioners, prophetesses – and, as such, *bearers of revelation*.

Without losing the challenging nature of Kristeva's insights, I need first to nuance her arguments from a historical perspective. Because she focuses so narrowly on the psychosexual development and oedipal conflicts of the child, the danger is that she ignores the diversity of social and historical roles which both motherhood and virginity have played, as well as the differences brought about by race, class and context. For example, consecrated virginity has in certain historical periods operated in a liberating way for women, allowing them a certain autonomy; and valorization in terms of other than child-bearing capacities. (Clearly this needs careful historical nuancing: monasticism frequently reproduced the same unjust power structures as the world which it had theoretically rejected.)

Similarly, the Gospel encounters of Jesus with women seem to imply a bursting-free from the bounds of patriarchy, even if in a limited sense. It is also generally recognized that the position of the great medieval abbesses allowed a tremendous degree of freedom and authority for women, even if this was largely restricted to upper-class women. The self-valuing of women as mothers also admits of huge cultural variations. If motherhood is to be explained solely in terms of the logic of sacrifice, 'God as Mother' would hardly be flourishing in Christian feminist circles as an illuminating image of God! For example, it is a European and middle-class tendency to protest against society's public/private split as damaging to women. In European womens' efforts to gain recognition outside the home, there is a tendency to downgrade the role within it. For many Third-World women – and very poor women in Euro-American society – the reverse is true. Where, in the wider society, only degrading and ill-paid jobs are available, women's only sense of being valued and having dignity may come from their home life as wives and mothers.

Again, Kristeva's focus on the psychoanalytic has narrowed her appreciation of Mary. Although women have suffered from the over-glorification of Mary, there *is* another discourse to be discovered – and feminist theology is very active in creating it.[34] This discourse has long been present in how the figure of Mary has worked in an inspirational and positive way in the lives of poor women. As was mentioned in the previous chapter, in connection with our Lady of Guadeloupe, women have long been able to relate to Mary as compassionate Mother, when the transcendent God and the divine Jesus seemed remote and alien. They also relate to her as a prophetic figure, as Goddess, as symbol of redeemed humanity.

Women do not only relate to Stabat Mater, to Mater Dolorosa, as expressive of the social contract of sacrifice and death, with a comforting vision of immortality. It is true that the affliction of Mary relates directly to the experience of many women throughout the world of being bowed down and crushed with suffering. But being crushed and passively acquiescing in suffering is not the deepest meaning of Mater Dolorosa. In Venezuela, in El Salvador and Argentina, in the

45

resistance and solidarity of women against oppression, it is frequently the figure of Mater Dolorosa, the mother grieving over her dead son, who inspires and fuels the struggle. Belief in resurrection, far from being a flight from life, or a counterfeit masculine consolation for death, in El Salvador actually *empowers* the earthly struggle.

ROMOLA AND A FLEXIBLE DISCOURSE FOR MOTHERHOOD

As a first step in reclaiming a more flexible discourse for motherhood – as part of moving us away from the 'mediated subjectivity' and logic of sacrifice in the story of Sonia – I end with the story of another woman, who achieved some degree of personal integrity and autonomy through motherhood. This is the story of Romola, by George Eliot (Marian Evans).[35] The novel is set in the Florence of the harsh Franciscan preacher Savanarola, and depicts the plight of Romola, a would-be scholar like so many of Eliot's heroines, betrayed by a fickle husband, Tito, from whom Romola tries in vain to escape.

In the context of the discussion here, what is significant is that she is brought back by Savanarola – who for her represents the whole force of Church tradition and patriarchal authority – to her essential duty to 'live the sacrifice' and return to the wretched marriage. There is no other alternative. Her awakening to a wider vision than the logic of sacrifice comes interestingly through the murder of her respected godfather, Bernardo del Nero (someone with whom she has no blood ties). In the most dramatic scene in the book she confronts Savanarola with a wider vision of justice:

> She spoke almost with bitterness:
> 'Do you, then, know so well what will further the coming of God's kingdom, father, that you will dare to despise the plea of mercy – of justice – of faithfulness to your own teaching?'
> 'And that is true!' said Savanarola with flashing eyes. . . . 'The cause of my party is the cause of God's Kingdom.'
> 'I do not believe it!' said Romola, her whole frame shaken with passionate repugnance. 'God's Kingdom is something wider – else, let me stand outside it with the beings that I love.'[36]

This awakening to a wider vision gives Romola the courage to break out of living the sacrifice and she leaves Tito and Florence, drifting down the river Arno to a plague-stricken village, to a kind of spiritual rebirth.

> She felt that she was in the grave, but not resting there: she was touching the hands of the beloved dead beside her, and trying to wake them.[37]

She is called to life again by the cry of a child, and is witness to what Eliot calls 'A deeper sympathy which even in its pains leaves a thirst that the Great Mother has no pains to still'.[38]

Romola becomes symbolically, in the eyes of the village people, the Holy Mother bearing milk to them. She who had walked away from her own miserable marriage now adopts a Jewish child, Benedetto ('the blessing'). In fact she becomes mother to the whole village, but her act is freely chosen. Freeing herself from living the sacrifice she can give expression to a profounder source of justice.

The next step is to try to discover a way to encapsulate this experience of a profounder source of truth, beauty, freedom and justice than is expressed by the symbolic, social contract. And to try to do this in a way faithful to the language of the body and the emotions; but also faithful to the sheer diversity of womens' experience, to its ambiguity and sometimes paradoxical nature, and to the difficulties of enunciation and articulation, given the prevailing understanding of what it means to be a human subject. Only then can we intuit a new understanding of revelation.

Cassandra,
Voice from the margins

Why did I want the gift of prophecy, come what may? To speak with my own voice, the ultimate. I did not want anything more, anything different.[1]

This is the voice of Sophia, in the shape of the tragic figure of Cassandra, speaking to us across the centuries as the prophetess doomed by Apollo never to be believed. She is the voice which would never be authentically heard. But this is no marginalized Sophia, beloved of society's outcasts, encountered only outside the prisons and around camp-fires. Cassandra is a royal princess, daughter of Priam, King of Troy, and reared in a militaristic culture, steeped in patriarchal values. At this point in the build-up of the argument Cassandra is needed, not as example of woman, outsider and invisible to the tradition – as was the case with Hagar – nor as example of mediated subjectivity (Sonia), nor as 'living the sacrifice' of becoming anonymous so as to procreate the species. Rather, Cassandra locates us at the heart of the obstacle to 'hearing revelation'. And here we have a philosophical dilemma. Her tragic situation is that she is poised at the interface of the dualist vision of western culture, intuiting another vision, scarcely able to express it, and doomed never to be 'heard' even if she finds a way to express it.

Here I do not approach Cassandra through the eyes of the Homeric poems or the tragic portraying of her in Aeschylus's *Oresteia* – where she is imaged as mad – but through the contemporary re-imaging of the German novelist and literary critic Christa Wolf.[2] Like Perceval this writer from the former East Germany seeks the right question to address to her own past, and gropes to express it with clarity. Cassandra encapsulates these efforts of women to find a voice and to give form to their struggles and experiences. Christa Wolf's Cassandra speaks from the writer's own contemporary context where Logos was developing his nuclear strength in East Germany after the Second World War. His discourse has become that of technological progress, whatever the cost in terms of human suffering. The Cassandra who struggles to find a voice today is poised between the collapse of communism and the alluring arms of capitalism. As yet she has not articulated a liberating language. To track the reasons for her inability to come to speech will involve turning upside-down our notions of human subjectivity – a kind of philosophical *Via Purgativa* (Method of Purification) – in order to be open to a new model of divine revelation.

The threat of nuclear war and the horrors of a post-war situation make the link between the historical context of Cassandra, Trojan princess, and our own. From childhood the young Cassandra was continually exposed to a patriarchal and militaristic set of values. She was a little girl who adored her father; yet her understanding and wisdom about the horrors of war grew from listening at her father's knee to all his councils of war. Devoted like any Trojan to the ancient city, she gradually became aware that there were values other than those of war-mongering and the sexual mores which surrounded her.

For her growing wisdom Cassandra was indebted to her nurse Parthena and the slave-woman, Marpessa. Here we see the underlying wisdom of Sophia, discovered among the poor and oppressed peoples – what Michel Foucault calls the 'subjugated knowledges'. This other set of values was given concrete expression by the community of women in the Scamander caves. Here flourished a peaceful, healing and creative community, devoted to the Mother Goddess Cybele. It was among these women that Cassandra knew her only happiness (that is, apart from her rather ambiguous relationship with Aeneas, the future founder of Rome).

We meet her (in Christa Wolf's account) when her life struggle is over, as she attempts to find some meaning from the recent catastrophic events. She is Agamemnon's captive, after the Trojans have lost the war, and is sitting in a cart outside his palace at Mycenae. Inside the Palace, Clytaemnestra, Agamemnon's wife, and her lover Aegisthus, are about to murder the returning king. After that it will be Cassandra's turn to die. It is at these last moments of her life that she 'sees' with utmost clarity:

> This is the secret that encircles and holds me together. Only here, at the utmost rim of my life, can I name it to myself. There is something of everyone in me, so I have belonged to no-one, and I have even understood their hatred of me.[3]

This is the final revelation – a connectedness with all people, which will be a central theme of this book. It is certainly not present when the young Cassandra, fresh from the discovery of her powers to see and hear the voice of the god, attempts to enunciate the 'truth' which she sees:

> A ring of silence descended around me. The palace, the place I called home, drew away from me; the inner courtyards I loved stopped speaking to me. I was alone with my justice.[4]

Cassandra had known her truth before she spoke it:

> I myself had known from the start. The voice that said this was a stranger's voice . . . I had set it free deliberately so that it would not tear me apart; I had no control over what would happen next.[5]

What happens next – as would happen at all the great crises of her life – are convulsions, darkness, paroxysms, partly because of being gripped by the great 'angst' of her knowledge, partly because of the pain of rejection of the society she lives in. It is this angst which makes it impossible to speak entirely with her own voice. It is angst caused by many factors, the most serious of which threatens her own self-understanding. It is angst, not just from horror at the greed, bestiality and cruelty of the conquerors, but at those willing to be their victims:

> What I did not understand then, and did not want to understand, was that many were prepared to be victims, not only from the outside, but through something in themselves. Everything in me revolted against that. Why?[6]

The feminist movement is very familiar with the resolution, 'This above all: to refuse to be victim'.[7] Cassandra's cry adds the insight that as long as one remains locked into the victim-oppressor way of reacting to life, the possibility of other liberating ways of being remains closed.

Because of Apollo's curse Cassandra does not have freedom to give external form to her inner experience. The curse is a mythological expression of the impossibility of breaking through the dominant way of thinking and speaking to offer another set of values. Cassandra becomes prey to *Ubereinstimmungssucht*, literally, 'agreement addiction'.[8] This is the weakness which leads to losing touch with authentic inwardness, to playing the game according to the rules, or even to play at being someone else, losing touch with one's own feeling. In fact this is Cassandra's comment on her brother Paris: 'Weak, brother. Weak. A weakling. *Hungry to conform.* Just look at yourself in the mirror'.[9]

The alternative to this temptation to conformity is *Fühlosigkeit*, or the state of not feeling. It is to block angst deliberately by blocking feeling: 'With satisfaction I felt the coldness spreading through me. I did not know that not to feel is never a step forward, scarcely a relief.'[10]

The sheer horror of what she sees, even before the war has broken out, overcomes Cassandra. She is alone in making the connections, in knowing the meaninglessness of the events about to unfold. She dares to name the truth that Helen of Troy did not actually exist, but was 'fictioned' as a pretext for war – as all wars must have a fictional pretext to disguise naked greed and the need to dominate. Overcoming the two ways of blocking her angst, she dares to give utterance:

> But I, I alone saw. Or did I really 'see'? What was it then? I felt? Experienced – yes, that's the word. For it was, yet it is, an experience when I 'see', when I 'saw'. Saw that the outcome of this hour was our destruction. Time stood still – the ultimate estrangement from myself and everyone . . . To be forced to give birth to what will destroy you: the terror beyond terror.[11]

What she saw brought Cassandra to the brink of revelation. Soon it seized her with full power. She must choose – kinship with the powerful, or loyalty to a deeper knowledge. This loyalty would challenge the way she thinks, speaks and feels, and would threaten the way she uses language. She can no longer use the word 'we'. For it is unclear who is to be included in the word 'we'. Gradually it becomes a more and more enfeebled 'we': for its use has threatened her ability to say 'I'.

This is revelation for her: she cannot now speak with her own voice. 'Who will find a voice again – and when?' is her cry just before death, in reaction to the knowledge that Agamemnon is about to be murdered.

The steps of the unfolding drama are well known. The grief of the Trojan people at the death of Hector, Cassandra's brother, at the hands of Achilles, 'the murdering beast', as well as his horrific murder and rape of Penthesilea, Queen of the Amazons, were the prelude to the entry of the famous 'horse' into the city. Cassandra's warnings – as ever – went unheeded. She herself was raped by Ajax, before being taken prisoner by Agamemnon. Far from being mad – as Aeschylus depicts her – in her final moments she attains a depth of 'seeing'.

Cassandra's struggles shed light on why it is so difficult to give credible utterance on the basis of a counter-cultural set of values. Her dilemma is acute. If she is to be true to the ground of her own experience by giving utterance to what she sees/feels/remembers (which are here the content of 'knowing') without falling into either 'agreement addiction' or 'feeling-lessness', she has to 'break, abandon, or expand some of the rules that govern our common language or behaviour'.[12] The real angst is the fear of losing one's own subjectivity through conformity to the social norm. (This was the fear that in the saying of 'we' the 'I' would be lost.) What is then the core of human subjectivity according to Cassandra? Why does her own self-understanding make it so difficult for her to be believed by others?

For Cassandra, openness to the divine, to see and hear the voice of god, is linked with understanding her own selfhood in a much more 'connected' manner. That is, her own experiences are given greater coherence by being interrelated with those of others. This is what Cassandra comes to understand by being alive:

To be able to give my inner picture of the world to others (to make others see what I see) is to make myself present, to be given in others' consciousness. I am altered by every new experience, every picture in me. To make others see what I see is therefore to alter the way I am given in their experience; to let myself be given differently by every experience. This is what Cassandra calls 'being live'.[13]

But the challenge of being true to her own insights and this enlarged meaning of experience will clash with the conventional norm. It means that she will be controlled and manipulated by those in power. It will condemn her – and anyone who tries to do the same – to live in angst. Living in angst is the only way of being true to the vision. Living in angst also involves pain, as Cassandra discovered when her deeper insights were rejected. She realized that what she had previously thought of as pain was nothing. To be able to name the pain was a step forward. Holding on to the vision is the only way to break out of the stifling underlying dualisms which have spawned our culture of violence.

Cassandra was able to break through to a vision beyond dualisms:

> For the Greeks there is no alternative but either truth or lies, right or wrong, outcry or defeat, friend or enemy, life or death. They think differently than we do. What cannot be seen, heard, smelled, heard, touched, does not exist. It is the other alternative that they crush between their clear-cut distinction, the third alternative, which in their view does not exist, the smiling vital force that is able to generate itself from itself over and over: the undivided spirit in life, life in spirit. Anchises, (father of Aeneas, Cassandra's lover), once said that empathy could be more important for the Greeks than the accursed invention of iron.[14]

In the eyes of Christa Wolf, this is where it becomes plain that the conflict between the Greeks and Trojans is merely one instance of the war game which 'civilization' has been playing since the recording of history, and which is particularly painfully exemplified in our own times. Cassandra's message is Christa Wolf's message, that there is a way of life beyond the polarities of the war games. But the joyous energy, the 'smiling vital force', obstructed by society's power games, is kept alive by the oppressed women who are excluded from them.

This is what Cassandra experienced briefly with the community in the Scamander caves. There she discovered an affection and joy which became channelled into artistic creativity, a legacy for future generations:

> We etched animals, people, ourselves inside the rock caves, which we sealed off before the Greeks came. We pressed our hands side by side into the soft clay. We called that imortalising our memory, and laughed. This turned into a touch-fest . . .[15]

Living in the shadow of death's imminence, believing in the freedom which comes from speaking with her own voice, will bring a deeper aloneness for Cassandra. For speaking with an 'ultimate voice' is to speak with such a breadth of perception that it would be almost impossible for others to follow her. She has now crossed the barriers between 'seeing' and 'knowing'. 'Knowing' is far deeper than the knowledge which can be expressed in formula, dogma or definition.

This is exactly the problem with which this book is grappling, in connection with the dogmatic expressions of divine revelation. Petra Von Morstein has evocatively summarized the difficulty: Cassandra's message is that

> . . . there cannot be human knowledge without individual experience, intensely felt, that every new experience disassociates us, me, from past and common knowledge. I am my experiences. My experiences are completely my own. My voice cannot be. It can necessarily be 'presque mienne' . . . A voice completely my own severs me from human community.[16]

The experience of speaking with one's own voice, which brings about severance from the human 'community', is shared by the painful experiences of those women and men throughout the centuries who have tried to speak out in the name of justice. Their voices must be silenced, as was that of Bishop Romero and the Jesuit martyrs of El Salvador. What is extraordinary is that contemporary Cassandras are cracking open the culture of silence and the stifling of the prophetic voice. The Korean theologian Professor Chung Hyun Kyung tells the story of Kwon-in-Sook, a 23-year-old labour activist, expelled from her university for her involvement in the student movement and then arrested as a subversive. When she refused to give names, the police sexually tortured her:

Ms Kwon was deeply humiliated . . . Her liberationist consciousness would not allow her to commit suicide. She decided to let the whole world know what she experienced. She wrote out a request to arrest the torturer. The request was discarded by the chief of security. Upon hearing of the incident, the women prisoners who were in the same prison as Ms Kwon went on a hunger strike to support her. The next day the male prisoners did the same.

This was the first time in history that a woman made a public issue of sexual violation . . . Ms Kwon broke the culture of silence on violations of women's sexual and personal integrity.[17]

Cassandra's seeing has given us insight about the qualitative otherness of the vision glimpsed beyond dualisms. In her struggle to keep alive the 'smiling vital force', a unity of experience and reason, *remaining connected to the ground of her experience*, and yet in connection with others, she has shown a way forward.

The Lion Gate at Mycenae stands silent today. It was the last sight of Cassandra before she died: 'The last sight will be a picture, not a word. Words die before pictures'.[18] But Cassandra's voice, after centuries of silence, is at last being heard into speech. A new discourse is being created.

4 Connectedness as New Metaphor for Christian Revelation

The world as it is: not as her users boast
damaged beyond reclamation by their using
Ourselves as we are in these painful motions

of staying cognizant: some part of us always
out beyond ourselves
knowing knowing knowing . . .

On a pure night on a night when pollution

seems absurdity when the undamaged planet seems to
turn
like a bowl of crystal in black ether
they are the piece of us that lies out there
knowing knowing knowing.

(Adrienne Rich, 'The Spirit of Place')[1]

BREAKTHROUGH TO ANOTHER PARADIGM?

Seeking new appreciation of divine communication today has entailed exposing the difficulties of traditional theories of Christian revelation as well as highlighting the central problem of the exclusion of women on which these have been built. But the inclusion of women within the social contract and the recovery of their voice within it has also been shown as fraught with difficulties: the logic of sacrifice and anonymity, the lurking ghost of essentialism and the dualistic framework of North American and European thought-patterns have all precluded the hearing of 'a different voice'. Nor is the fact of marginal status any guarantee that the voice which is 'heard into speech' will have a superior claim to 'truth' or divine origin.

No mystique should be woven around marginal status itself, or around the exclusion of oppressed groups from positions of authority. Rather, through listening to Cassandra's voice (understood as the prophetic voice ignored by the dominant

57

culture), we hope to break through to another paradigm or way of understanding God's communication. Through the discovery of a new philosophical underpinning or dominant metaphor for the way we 'receive' the world, we can move to a deeper experience of God's relationship with us and with the whole of creation.

Contextual theology and social analysis teach us the limitations of any one perspective. We now make more modest claims, in awareness of the pitfalls of all-embracing, universalistic theories. Social background, differing degrees of privilege and power, race, gender, sexual preference, education and health are only some of the factors influencing the stance we take. Yet it is still important to take a stance, while admitting its limitations; both the shortcomings of which we are aware, and history's verdict (as yet unknown). Sitting on the philosophical and theological fence has never made any contribution to human development; taking a stance, while recognizing the limitations of a perspective, may actually free some space for other voices, particularly for those as yet unheard.

The inspiration for this particular metaphor springs from its rootedness in the mutual interaction of feminist liberation movements with long-hidden strands of Christian theology. The goal of the former has always been the liberation of women – on a global basis. 'Till all women are free, then no woman is free', is a well-known slogan. The goal of Christian feminism is the transformation of relationships between men and women within a renewed understanding of the whole of creation. To that end Christian feminists focus on the exposing and eradicating of the mutually interacting oppressions of race, class and sex, through the weeding out of oppressive elements from our religious tradition and the articulation of a liberating vision. This vision arises from both a heightened consciousness and a commitment to transformative action. It also arises from within the creation of a new culture, life-style and the mushrooming of new communities based on its commitment and praxis.

Thus the promise of the paradigm offered will be measured by its ability to enhance the transformed relations of women and men within the wider whole, and its potential for inspiring a liberating praxis. What this means, practically, is that even if this metaphor is being articulated from within a European context, with all that is entailed in terms of privilege and the history and legacy of cultural and political imperialism, yet it is a metaphor constantly vulnerable: it remains open to the crucible of experience. Does the metaphor inspire the 'power that drives to justice'? Is it of mere transient significance? Its ability to function as a *metaphor for revelation* will stand or fall according to its fruitfulness in empowering Christian communities to enter more deeply into communication with God, or to rediscover a source of communication, hidden by layers of distorted dualisms.

The metaphor of connectedness has become central for the womens' movement and for Christian feminist spirituality, as well as playing an increasingly dynamic role in ecological circles. In the sixties the slogan 'the solidarity of sisterhood' was powerful, even if its rhetoric has now been challenged.[2] In fact, I see some of the difficulties and challenges which we now face as being another phase of the movement, *not* as an indication of its failure. But 'solidarity in the struggle' means more than resistance. The centrality of a new way of relating has become a dominant focus. We speak now of 'mutuality-in-relation', of overcoming relationships based on hierarchical dominance/submission patterns with relationships of reciprocity, interdependence and mutuality. 'Compassionate empathy' is seen to inspire a new way of being in the world, even if the dangers of falling into a new essentialism and universalism must be avoided.

Carter Heyward, a pioneer of relational theology within North American Christian feminism, re-imaged God as 'power-in-relation'.[3] In *Redeeming the Dream* I attempted to understand Christian redemption as making right relation.[4] To be redeemed is to build right relation, to claim power-in-relation in the praxis of liberation here and now. Others use the metaphor of energy or connection. Catherine Keller, for example, sees God as the source of connection.[5] Here I deliberately use the metaphor of 'connectedness' or 'interconnectedness' rather than 'relationality' or interrelatedness because of its potential for greater inclusivity. 'Relatedness' or 'mutuality-in-relating' gives the impression that we are only talking about men and women: but theology must be inclusive

of the whole of creation. Christian feminist theologians are not
the only people working along these lines: we share insights
from and with current ecological thinking, creation theology,
organic philosophy (including process philosophy), the rediscovery of relationship with nature in pastoral counselling, as
well as some creative thinking about relationality.[6] *This is part
of the meaning of divine revelation – that it is being poured out
ceaselessly, the beauty ancient and new, shedding new light on
experience, and putting our Christian history and tradition under
a new sense of judgement from a liberation theology perspective.*

We need a clear starting-point, a view of both self and world
which explores connection while respecting difference. Most
important for this work will be to listen to voices from other
cultures, especially to those of Third-World women, in all
their specificity, particularly in the critique offered to western
theology. I begin with the visionary promise of the metaphor.

EPIPHANIES OF CONNECTION FROM A BROKEN WORLD

Any connecting we do has to be re-connecting. Rita Brock in
her book *Journeys by Heart* pictures the world as broken-
hearted. For her, the notion of 'heart' is crucial to draw us back
to original integrity.[7] In our broken-hearted world we are
threatened and overwhelmed by broken connections. We find
it difficult – even if we get the theory right – to live in a way
which respects both mind and body. We want to re-connect
with the natural world, yet drown in our exhaust fumes and
poison ourselves slowly by what we eat and drink. This is
without mentioning our failure to make the connection
between our consumptive life-styles and the destruction of the
environment. The reality of a sexual relationship may be more
a sea of separation than a genuine connecting, so far are human
beings estranged from a genuine ground for relating. Politically,
we have never been so well-informed about the injustices of
the South–North divide, but this knowledge has not transformed
our patterns of connecting. We seem to be paralysed in our
disconnection and misconnection.

Catherine Keller uses spider imagery to inspire the task of
re-connection. The Spider Goddess, Arachne (from a Greek

legend), presents a great epiphany of making connections, yet spins from a broken web[8] – a web referred to by Jean Sinday as the spider's web of triple oppression (racism, classism, sexism). As Adrienne Rich writes:

> Anger and tenderness: the spider's genius
> To spin and weave in the same action
> from her own body, anywhere –
> even from a broken web.[9]

The same task is expressed theologically by those process theologians who link the creative and redemptive moments as two aspects of the same process.

The notion of 'epiphanies of connection' is found in the work of many women novelists, from George Eliot to Alice Walker, offering a range of interpretations for the idea. The dimension of connectedness with the natural world is prominent.[10] The challenge to rediscover interconnectedness with the natural world is now embraced as an *ethical* task by ecological groups the world over but has yet to be recognized as a priority on the agenda of the world faiths, despite the persevering efforts of a few individuals.

As I write, today is the feast of Epiphany. This is the feast above all which for Christians tells of God's love poured out for the whole world, of the many Holy Fools (the wise people of God) who have set out on the search for wisdom. Epiphany has inspired a whole literary genre where a moment of experience takes on ultimate and transcendent significance.[11]

Within Christian theology interconnectedness with the whole of creation has been a well-buried strand, suffocated in the tradition through hierarchical dualisms, as Catharina Halkes has shown us in her latest book.[12] Eco-feminist theologian Anne Primavesi has for the first time attempted a systematic re-evaluation of creation theology from the perspective of the essential inter-relatedness of all creation, in her book *From Apocalypse to Genesis*.[13] The call for a renewed theology of creation, which will replace an anthropocentric focus with one of interconnection, has become insistent.[14]

If interconnectedness is to be seen as an epiphany of divine communication, it must include more than a recovery of interdependence with the natural world and the despised homely wisdoms, even though these are important dimensions. For one thing, recovery of connection brings the revelation of damaging and destructive connection. Fires blaze in the Gulf, and black snow falls in the Himalayas. Nuclear bombs explode in the Pacific and women give birth to malformed babies. Merely 'making the connection' without facing the ethical implications which accompany the insight brings no transformation. The connectedness we seek, far from being a middle-class flight into 'pure nature' as refuge from demonic technocracy, seeks to transform technology's relationship with the environment.

Re-connecting – earlier I called this 'redeeming the connections'[15] – claims to be *divine*, because it is re-rooting in the basic relational energy of the universe. It is how we recover our energy and creativity, for our present situation, *in contact with sustaining and nurturing memories from the past*.

This is how I want to re-image a relationship with Christian tradition – as nurturing and sustaining memory. Thus faith in the present experience of divine relational power, from the mutual interaction of the liberation struggles and the Christian story, casts suspicion over the way in which this tradition has been handed on. It fuels a quest for a relational understanding of revelation, for the posing of questions which elicit from the sources ways of energizing us in our ethical quest. It casts suspicion also on the gaps and chasms in the texts. (This is not to criticize a text for what we would have preferred it to say: a text has its own integrity. But it is to challenge the hierarchical, excluding mechanisms which interpret the way God's communication is transmitted, in the hope of liberating the text for inclusive interpretations.) Elisabeth Schüssler Fiorenza has already challenged us to reclaim the background of the New Testament, but not as background: rather that women with their experiences and theological reflection should be reclaimed for the centre.[16] I want to extend this attempt to the whole of the tradition-forming process, and to respond to the need to interpret the core of theological reflection with the dynamism of the metaphor of interconnectedness.

I am using 'text' in a very wide sense. By text I mean the dominant interpretations of Christian doctrines as expressed in dogmas, theological textbooks, the catechisms by which they are communicated to the people as a whole, the spiritualities which they engender, the stream of papal encyclicals and apostolic letters which attempt to control their interpretation; I also mean the whole world of image and symbol, conscious and unconscious through which faith is expressed. 'Text' means also the music and poetry, image, sculpture, film and play which both reflect and influence our beliefs, and represent the interface and interrelation between the faith story and the cultural story as a whole. It will already be clear, from the emphasis I have been placing on bringing the margin to the centre, that I hope to bring many sub-texts into consideration, and to enter into a listening dialogue with discourses forgotten, ignored or as yet undiscovered.

As a hermeneutic key to the 'text of Christian revelation' for the dimension of connectedness I explore, apart from the feminist theological sources mentioned above, I use both the contemporary literature of black women and the theological works of Asian and African women theologians. I regard these as inspirational sources and wish to place them centrally, with full respect for their contextual implications and the implicit and explicit critique they carry for European and North American culture.

First, Alice Walker's novel *Meridian* provides a treasury of examples of what I mean by the revelatory quality 'redeeming connectedness' which includes a recovery of connection with creation – and takes us much further. When the protagonist, Meridian, is a college student, an ancient tree, the Sojourner, provides a uniting focus for the black students. In the tragic story of the uncivilized, despised and pregnant Wild Child, whom Meridian had tried to befriend and who was refused Christian burial by the college chapel, it is the Sojourner's branches which receive the funeral casket:

> Then, as if by mutual agreement . . . the pallbearers picked up the casket and put it gently down beneath the Sojourner, whose heavy, flower-lit leaves, hovered over it like the inverted peaks of a mother's half-straightened kinky hair. Instead of flowers the students, as if they had planned it, quickly made wreaths from Sojourner's fallen leaves, and the Sojourner herself, ever generous to her children, dropped a leaf on the chest of the Wild Child, who wore for the first time, in her casket, a set of new clothes.[17]

63

In one fell swoop this story reveals the strength of the tree as far from a recovery of connection with idealized nature; the tree offers 'redeeming connection', a focus for this community's grief which the human (white and Christian) community has refused. But it is a link with more than nature: the tree is *the locus of community memory*, a veritable storehouse of memory and hope. Tragically, despite Meridian's entreaties, the grieving, frustrated students end the day by rioting and sawing down the tree, 'that mighty, ancient, sheltering music tree'.[18]

A similar tree provides solace for Jadine, the central character of Toni Morrison's *Tar Baby*. At the biggest crisis of her life Jadine thought of

> . . . a towering brass beech – the biggest and oldest in the state. It stood on the north side of the campus and near it was a well. In April the girls met their mothers there to sing and hold hands and sway in the afternoon light . . . Some of the girls hated it . . . and sat around in jeans and no shoes smoking herb to show their contempt for bourgeoisie sentiment . . . But the girls who did not hate it surrounded the beech and in long pastel shirts swayed in the spring light.[19]

Through the image of the tree (and the memory of an earlier tree which had saved her from the island swamp), Jadine discovers a way to find new connections with women, and to reject earlier, inappropriate models. She finds a benevolent maternal image through which she discards more regressive female models.

But it is again Meridian who reveals how the metaphor qualifies as revelatory. Through re-connecting with her father's grandmother, the Indian Feather Mae, she attains her own experience of religious ecstasy and exaltation. Feather Mae had experienced physical ecstasy at the ancient Indian burial ground known as the Sacred Serpent. It was here that Meridian went:

> Seeking to understand her great-grandmother's ecstasy and her father's compassion for people dead centuries before he was born, she watched him enter the deep well of the Serpent's coiled tail and return to his cornfield with his whole frame radiating brightness like the space around a flame.[20]

And then it happens to Meridian herself:

But it was in her head that the lightness started. It was as if the walls of earth that enclosed her rushed outward, levelling themselves at a dizzying rate, and then spinning wildly, lifting her out of her body, and giving her the feeling of flying. And in this movement she saw the faces of her family, the branches of trees, the wings of birds, the corners of houses, blades of grass and petals of flowers rush towards a central point high above her, and she was drawn with them.[21]

The point here is not so much to emphasize an out-of-body mystical experience, where this seems to match 'classical' parallels; rather that the ecstasy of connecting with all living things and people brought with it an expansion of consciousness of being alive – and this, in a place sacred to the memory of the dead. Meridian experiences the same expansion of connection on a mountain in Mexico:

There would again be a rushing out from her all that was surrounding, all that she might have touched, and again she would become a speck in the grand movement of time. When she stepped upon the earth again it would be to feel the bottoms of her feet curl over the grass, as if her feet were those of a leopard or a bear.[22]

For these women, re-connecting with traditions submerged in a dominant culture, recovering nature as strength, re-membering community values which sustain them in the current struggle, were all integral parts of their communication with the divine.

That 'epiphanies of connections' can offer a hermeneutic key to Christian revelation is also shown by voices emerging from Asian, African and Latin-American theology of women in struggle. Their voices and witness reveal that a metaphor of connection, far from being a metaphor only for the privileged, is a necessary pre-condition for future survival and well-being. As Chung Hyun Kyung writes:

Asian women know they cannot endure meaningless suffering if they do not dream of a world defined by wholeness, justice and peace. They also know that they will perish without a vision of life in its fullness and in its deepest beauty.[23]

This 'vision of life in its fullness' which elsewhere she posits as the basis of a 'life-centred culture',[24] is inspired by an image of God as 'a life-giving Spirit they (Asian women) encounter in

65

themselves and *in everything which fosters life* (my italics) . . .
God as life-giving spirit is present everywhere and moves
everywhere.'[25]

The image of an immanent God energizing Asian women's
journey to wholeness is shown by Marta Benavides, a woman
theologian from El Salvador, to be part of a 'connection' view
of creation where care for the Garden of Creation is linked with
solidarity and a commitment to justice-making on this earth:

> To garden with others is an expression of solidarity; that is what
> being 'companeras' is all about. Gardening is visioning, dreaming,
> and futuring for me too. But I cannot bring about the new earth by
> myself, because a new earth demands that we look at the universe
> in which we are immersed. We must look for the new we are
> called to bring forth. We must see what is old and decadent and
> death-giving . . . (p. 134).
>
> The garden I inherited from my mother has become for me the
> whole of creation. We all need to join together to live as
> 'companeras' and tend the global garden . . . We must . . . make
> real connections between the gardens of El Salvador, Central
> America and the whole world. I am one with my nation just as the
> plants and flowers are one with the soil. But the soil of El Salvador
> has been plundered, and there is almost nothing for us to inherit.[26]

It is significant to me that the holistic, inclusive view of
creation is coming so strongly from the literature and theology
of Third-World women, who themselves are suffering so
severely from the triple oppressions of racism, sexism and
poverty. It suggests not only that the comparatively privileged
position of western women stultifies an openness to new
visions, but also that the European predominant view of
subjectivity is a barrier to this, and needs to be challenged.

It is to the development of a new sense of self within a
metaphor of connection that I now turn.

5 The Separate Self and the Denial of Relation

> We know now we have always been in danger
> down in our separateness
> and now up here together but till now
> we had not touched our strength
> (Adrienne Rich, 'Phantasia for Elvira Shatayev')[1]

How do we understand our own individuality? Adrienne Rich evokes here the stark nature of the current predicament. What overwhelms us too often is compassion-fatigue, inertia, the inability of the prevailing ethic to change anything. Neither reasoned analysis nor response to catastrophes based on the generosity of a few individuals appears to be able to shift the grip of unjust systems on a global scale or prevent the suffering they bring about. Any 'drive to connect' takes place amid the brokenheartedness of oppressed communities and crucified peoples. It is a brokenheartedness caused partially by a *structured separateness*. If this sounds an exaggerated claim, think of the way we organize our world, our institutions and our relationships, following in part from the way we understand the human person. To what degree are all of these structured by the notion of separation and, on the level of subjectivity, by separative individualism and its far-reaching consequences? 'The individual deserves what he gets and gets what he deserves' is still a very popular slogan.

This is why the political and social transformation must first be on the level of our philosophical consciousness and symbolic order. Invitations to connect, re-connect, or build relationships around the notion of mutuality will make no difference until the all-pervasiveness of the notion of separation – even within theology itself – is recognized, together with the difficulties of moving away from this to re-structure on the basis of connection: *to discover 'the connected self' in a connected world.*

Is it possible to develop a way of doing theology to overcome separative individualism, and to develop an understanding of

67

the connective self which still affirms and celebrates otherness? Is it possible to develop a pluralist notion of selfhood which refuses to reduce the other to the dominant model of selfhood? As far as tracing the historico-philosophical development of this, feminist theology owes a debt to the inspirational work of Catherine Keller. In *From a Broken Web*[2] Keller does not rest with identifying the roots of the 'separate self' in philosophy and theology, but assembles resources for creative thinking on the self around the notion of connection.

Charles Taylor, in his illuminating *Sources of the Self*, indicates key moments in the development of the modern self within European thought.[3] The ideas of Descartes and Locke, of the human subject as a *disengaged individual*, were highly influential for the dominant European notion of the self – the kind of self-awareness of Logos in chapter 1. (Not that it solves the problem to begin scapegoating particular individuals: these ideas were influential because they arose from and responded to the contemporary climate of understanding.) Whatever influences are identified as contributing to how we understand the modern identity – the legacy of Platonic dualism, capitalism, romanticism, empiricism, and so on – the point here is that these can be grouped around the pivotal points of 'distance', 'separation' and 'detachment'. I have already stressed the absence of women from the process of defining the human subject, a fact now being addressed by contemporary psychology, anthropology and sociology. The modern (male) subject who has been defined from positions of power – the European hero, conquistador, pirate rather than his victim – dominates the classic definition of the subject. It has been a very *Christian* imperialistic notion of subjectivity, either oblivious to or distinguishing itself from, other discourses within its midst.

Here the discussion shifts from the usual feminist stance which seeks (quite rightly) to overcome hierarchical dualisms in the name of achieving equal status for women. This is because we need to ask, *On what basis are we to re-organize?* The state of the debate as to feminist identity seems to me to be deadlocked at the moment. There has been a movement both forward and away from the sixties' struggle to prove that women were no different from men, should not be identified by biological determinism, and were equal to any task. Now the question of difference has reappeared, particularly on the French scene.[4] Women, it is argued, have different experiences, have a different cultural heritage, possibly different strengths and weaknesses – although this is a controversial area. But how is this difference to be defined, without pushing us back to another version of the old essentialism? This is the current dilemma. I raise this here because it seems that in the effort to resist the oppression caused by crushing dualisms, or simply the exclusion of women from the full benefits of being human subjects, we (in western culture at least) fall into the same trap of taking on the same notions of separative individualism which have so oppressed us. The Logos of chapter 1 – whom we will re-encounter – is not just a male figure. There are plenty of examples of dominating and exploitative women.

To grasp the way in which separative individualism has structured how we understand ourselves we have to bring to the light not merely contemporary socio-cultural patterns, but their mythological underpinnings. What are the formative stories which support our notions of the human person? We need to become sensitive to the way our culture has used the hero-concept, so prominent in these stories, even in the 'texts' of Christian revelation (which I will show in a later chapter), so that it bolsters the authority of separative individualism.

The pattern of the classic hero-epic is illustrated by the Homeric hero Odysseus and his wife Penelope, who is left behind on the island of Ithaca. Odysseus wanders, has adventures, achieves and conquers, while Penelope keeps the home fires burning – and weaves. But this is no creative spinning of new connections, no creative waiting, but an apathetic 'time-filler': for in the night she unravels and starts again. The hero's exploits are based on distancing himself from the home base and on external achievements of a military nature. Becoming a self seems more a matter of external activity: interiority disappears, or is transposed onto the supernatural level. The hero literally makes his imprint on the external world through conquest, piracy and constructing empires, and, as we shall see, through the abandonment of intimate relation. (The contemporary equivalent is the travelling company executive, although this is changing because of computer-techniques: the hero does not now need to move from his desk in order to achieve his goal.) Lest it be thought that this criticism is only applicable to a small segment of human experience which demands a degree of mobility destructive of personal bonding, the gender distinction which George Steiner makes with regard to artistic creativity shows how widespread this blindness is. There is, he claims, 'a gender-bias in any model of creation as agonistic, as an act of wrestling with, against the 'other maker'.[5] Women, he feels, find the biological act of giving birth so fulfilling that this renders 'comparatively pallid, the begetting [*sic*] of fictive personae which is the matter of drama and so much representative art'.[6] Women are so in touch with the holiness of being that they feel no impulse to rival the jealous God, to fight the terrible Angel!

While Steiner's biological determinism allows him to claim real acts of creation as masculine because of their alleged 'agonistic' character (women being supposedly in harmony with holy being), the legendary hero's achievements are made possible by the acquiescence of women in keeping the hearth. Indeed, the stories make it clear that women get in the way of the hero's quest (except as a victim to be rescued). Prince Aeneas of Troy left his wife Creusa in the flames of the burning city because of his divine-sent mission to found a new dynasty – the city of Rome. This is not the only woman he abandoned. Falling in love with Dido, Queen of Carthage, at a later stage in his adventures, she too must be cast aside, weeping, on the shore.

It seems that commitment-in-relationship cannot be combined with divinely-given destiny. How deep the chasm is between the two ways of understanding the world – through connectedness or through the logic of (heroic) individualism – is immortalized by Virgil, when he describes the encounter of Aeneas with Dido in the underworld: 'I could not believe', he tells her, 'that I would hurt you so terribly.' He even weeps when he sees the wound of her suicide, asking 'Was I the cause?'

The psychologist Carol Gilligan – well-known for her work in uncovering 'another voice' in moral discourse[7] – has used this story to illustrate the moral ambiguity of our western tradition: Aeneas describes himself as a man set apart, bounded by his responsibility to his destiny. Caught between two images of himself – as implicated and as innocent, as responsible and as tossed about by fate – he exemplifies the dilemma of how to think about the self, how to represent the experience of being at once separated and connected to others through a fabric of human relationship.[8]

Gilligan claims that the two images of self anchored in these two conceptual frameworks imply two ways of thinking about responsibility which are fundamentally incompatible:

> The detachment of Aeneas's 'pietas' becomes the condition for his ignorance of her feelings; yet his adherence to his mission does not imply the indifference that she in her responsiveness imagined. Thus, the simple judgment that would condemn Aeneas for turning away from Dido or Dido for breaking her vow of chastity yields to a more complex vision – one that encompasses the capacity for sustained commitment and the capacity for responsiveness in relationships and recognizes their tragic conflict.[9]

For me this story conveys not only the impression of the fragility of loving relationships and their vulnerability to loss and separation; it also raises the dilemma that moral obligation, as we have come to understand it, necessarily requires detachment and separation. And the more the destiny is understood as divinely-imposed, the greater the separation involved. *Without the notion of separation, our whole ethical discourse collapses like a pack of cards.* And this is a terrifying thought.

Lest it be imagined that this ethic of stoic detachment and separation belongs merely to ancient Greece and Rome, let us remember that the language of celibacy and priesthood of Christianity has up until recently insisted on separation from the female world. Perceval's farewell to his mother has been repeated in the numerous young men whose ties with home had to be broken in order to free them for God's service. As a child I could never understand why my young brother, who entered a Junior Seminary for the priesthood, was only allowed to come home *after* Christmas, and *after* Easter, for me the high point of our family life. When visiting him I was soon aware of the averted eyes of his fellow seminarians – a rude awakening to the way seminary education of the time regarded

71

the presence of women. That certain 'privileged' women were allowed to enter the discourse of separation is illustrated by the story of the widow Paula and St Jerome. To achieve sanctity she was encouraged by him to deny her femininity (become an 'honorary man', in other words) by embracing consecrated monastic celibacy and abandoning her children. The account of the children standing weeping on the shore as their mother's boat disappeared makes chilling reading.[10]

Nor could I understand why the public school system encouraged boys from the age of eight into its preparatory schools, or why parents acquiesced in keeping the system going. Independence, detachment and objectivity, control of the emotions, love of an ordered, stratified society, and emphasis on individual achievement, are all much-admired qualities, which depend on the suppression of a relational world-view. Even the more 'progressive' contemporary Christian spirituality can encourage this value-system. 'Virtue' – itself a male-oriented word (deriving from Latin *vir* = man) – is still described as a quality of an individual which is to be cultivated as part of the path to holiness. The spiritual journey is still imaged as the fraught path of the lonely hero who has to undergo trials and tribulations to attain sanctity. *Renunciation is lauded above appreciation, sacrifice more than participation, sexual abstinence more than responsible enjoyment. Relational commitment as a vital part of spiritual journeying has no place.* If we then reflect that the logic of separation underpins medical, educational and industrial structures, we begin to see its far-reaching, damaging effects.

But it is in the prison system and in making war where separation as punishment is taken to its ultimate extreme. The prisoner is separated from the human community, his or her world deliberately reduced to a cell, often in solitary confinement where connectedness is systematically destroyed, from motives of either punishment or (in name) deterrence. Elaine Scarry, in a book full of insights (*The Body in Pain: the Making and Unmaking of the World*)[11] shows, through the example of war and torture, exactly what are the structures of making and unmaking involved. She shows how the process of torture literally uncreates the human person. The prisoner's language and voice are destroyed. The pain of the prisoner is denied reality and transformed into the power of the interrogator. The prisoner is systematically un-made, in a manner which mimics the structures of making and creating. The prisoner's whole world is destroyed and s/he becomes all body – the body in pain – whereas the interrogator becomes all voice. This is a horrible parody of the book of Genesis, where the voice of God creates, summoning the body into being and sentience.

If we examine the greatest political and racial oppositions of the world, they can be understood as many interlocking forms of separation. Racial, economic and religious divisions interpenetrate and fester. The word 'separatist' – Basque separatist, Tamil separatist, and so on – usually refers to a minority group, desperate for recognition of its own identity, which is scarcely acknowledged to exist by the dominant group.

Finally, the activity of making war – at bottom an activity of out-injuring the other – demands that I see the other as separate, as 'threatening other', over against me and totally disconnected from me. The denial of relation has to be pushed to extremity to permit systematic slaughter, even to the extremes of genocide, as the Holocaust and the Vietnam War remind us.

It is in the area of health care, interestingly, that the logic of separation is beginning to break down. People in hospitals are rebelling at being solely identified by their diseased organ – the stomach in bed nine – and in any case this attitude has not by and large produced health. (I do not for a moment want to underestimate the devoted care of nurses who try to counteract this model.) People are flocking to hospices for the terminally ill, where these are available, where they are treated with dignity as whole persons in their family situations. Acupuncture, holistic medicine, attention to diet and life-style are all ways in which we are seeking to recover connection with ourselves as whole people-in-relationship. Questions on both local and international levels are posed as to the social and political causes of disease. The notion that good health care should be a question of privilege and money is at least theoretically disputed.

This is made possible by replacing a logic of separation with a metaphysic of connection.

TOUCHING OUR STRENGTH: THE RE-IMAGING OF THE SELF THROUGH THE DYNAMICS OF CONNECTION

A metaphysic of connection grounds itself on a view of the world as relational: within this view the human person is re-imaged in a more interconnected and interdependent manner. That is, the growth towards fullness of personhood, in all its biological and cultural specificity, is dependent on the dynamics of interconnection rather than on those of detachment and separation. This book is exploring the potential of this as a metaphor for Christian revelation. Metaphor, symbol and image are the most effective tools, rather than the trend of theology which works with models (see the account of Dulles' models of revelation in chapter 2), because a model carries with it more the implication of workable hypothesis, open to empirical confirmation or refutation, and thus the very severe notion of detachment and distance from which I am trying to escape. I want to find a way of re-envisioning these basic splits in a way which overcomes the traditional distance between the rational subject and the world he researches as object.

Catherine Keller attempted to develop a widened understanding of the human subject, using concepts of the social self and the process view of the world of Alfred North Whitehead. Although I make use of a process framework I do it cautiously, now far more aware of the problems than previously.[12] In fact, thinking non-dualistically is the aim of many contemporary writers committed to the well-being of the planet. We can even speak about an 'archaeology' of non-dualistic ancestry, in the sense which Michel Foucault employs. From Martin Buber's concept of the mutuality of 'I and Thou' as a way of relating, from systems theory – in which the world is seen as a complex of mutually interacting eco-systems – the theories of some contemporary physicists,[13] the intimations of poets and mystics, and especially from the work of eco-feminists and ecological theologians like Edward Echlin and Thomas Berry,[14] we see an emergent world-view based on connectedness. The damage inflicted on our consciousness by the logic of separation requires that all these attempts be given coherence and systematic reflection within Christian theology. Music has

74

given us Haydn's Creation, Beethoven's Pastoral Symphony, Mahler's Resurrection; but theology still remains locked into structures of distance and 'otherness'. *Das Ganze Andere* (the Wholly Other) of Rudolph Otto and Karl Barth still functions as the preferred description for the Godhead and, by derivation, 'the other' as our way of describing human personality. What is required is neither the elimination of 'the other', or retention of 'the other' as dominant category, but *respect for and commitment to the well-being of the other in her/his gendered subjectivity and socio-cultural context.*

CONNECTED SELF, ECOLOGICAL SELF

The first step in such a process is to see ourselves with new eyes. I re-image myself not as an individual defined over against another, but in-relation-to, connected-with. My own becoming is a many-levelled process not just in connection with the people I relate to, the political and social structures which shape my possibilities, the efforts I make to stay rooted in the rhythms of creation, but in the way I am able to use this dynamic of interconnectedness as key to personal growth and self-understanding. How can I integrate body/mind/heart/soul/sexual feeling within a wholeness of relational self-understanding? How can I connect with my authentic community group – nation, cultural group, religious tradition – in a way which both contributes to and draws strength from community memory, purpose and celebration, and yet remains receptive to and affirming of other communities?

To achieve this process of becoming a self, the 'I' must itself be seen as looser, more fluid, and relational in basic self-understanding. We need to re-examine the models of child-development which have been handed on to us as normative. Not only are they frequently gender-insensitive, but they also rely on the notion of separation as crucial for personality development. As I showed in chapter 3, when discussing the sacrificed subjectivity of women, according to Julia Kristeva, it was deemed necessary for the young child (= boy) to separate from the body of the archaic, instinctual mother in order to establish himself in the social contract and to survive in the public world. Numerous initiation rites of young males into

75

full membership of the tribe involve a ritual death to the world of the female. Return to the tribe involves literal separation from female presence and values. What is most damaging as regards western self-identity is the way adulthood has become synonymous with control, an ego-integrity which denies connectivity, and which depends on seeing the world as radically separate. It is this disengaged individual, as Keller points out, who is the real narcissist:

> The narcissist never encounters the objectivity, the acute difference of the other, but uses the other for self-gratification. The world is the mirror of the narcissist. But things are quite the reverse for the connective self. This self mirrors the world. . . . Is the Cartesian ego, with its splendidly separate sense of self, not an idealised self-image of the narcissist?[15]

Thus Keller answers the frequent charge against connectivity that, because 'all is connection', distinction becomes impossible. It is a criticism against connection theology that we are in peril of drowning in a sea of relation. We will merge into each other and lose both all clear sense of our own identity, as well as appreciation of the cultural and economic contexts of the other. It will be impossible to discern, it is argued, where I stop and another begins. And this weak or mediated sense of self, as Jean Baker Miller and psychologists of the Stone Centre for Human Development have frequently pointed out, has often led women to sacrifice any sense of self in service of others.[16] But this happens *not* because of viewing the world and ourselves as interconnected, but because of the sheer power of the prevailing concept of identity, and structures built around it. We are born to a culture fed on the myth of the survival of the fittest, which condones the violence inflicted by the powerful in order to maintain their positions. This is the culture which finds difference a threat and tries to reduce connectivity to conformity. But why not allow the glorious diversity of connectedness full rein and see what could happen, for example, to the debates on Church 'unity'? The reason for the current stalemate, it seems to me, is that our imagination is stultified through *reductive models of conformity*. Recognizing our connectedness with each other, far from suppressing difference, empowers us to welcome diversity and to interact creatively with its social and political consequences. *On the basis of connection, we value difference.*

The notion of the connected self is event, process and task. But the process is far from a fluid, steady movement towards greater harmony. Process thought frequently appears to be the child of cheery optimism – perhaps the heir to the nineteenth-century love of universality and the abstraction of the grand systems. At this juncture we are more aware of partial solutions and of the limits of context and ambiguity.[17] This becomes clear when we use the term 'ecological self' to describe the process of making connections. The term originates within the ecology movement and within systems theory. It links the abstraction of the separate self, this false reification of the 'I', with the current ecological crisis. In fact, Joanna Macy, in a moving article, 'Awakening to the Ecological Self', quotes Gregory Bateson as calling this false reification 'the epistemological fallacy of the Occidental civilisation'. He locates the self in a much larger trial-and-error system, which does the thinking, acting and deciding. Joanna Macy writes:

> We have imagined that the unit of survival, as Bateson puts it, is the separate individual, or the separate species. In reality, as throughout the history of evolution, it is the individual plus environment, the species plus environment, for they are essentially symbiotic.[18]

Although systems theory invites us to align our identity within a larger 'pattern that connects', this does not involve an eclipse of the distinctiveness of one's own experience. Our diversities do not merge and dissolve. Rather, says Macy, integration and differentiation go hand in hand. For her, this is expressed theologically by the Buddhist image of 'The Boundless Heart of the Bodhisattva'.[19] Here the notion of the abiding, individual self is seen as one of the foundational delusions of modern thought. The doctrine of 'no-self' can liberate us from the rat-race of chasing our own delusions, of being propelled by our own greed. The boundless heart image can transform our individualist egos, and refocus us round a larger centre. It can inspire both a new ethics and a new way of knowing. In Hua Yen Buddhism the image of connective inter-dependence is the 'jewelled net of Indra'. This is a cosmic canopy, 'where each of us, each jewel at each node of the net, reflects all of the others and reflects the others reflecting back'.[20]

Discovering the pattern that connects, and that human subjectivity is interconnected with non-human processes and rhythms, is not a tidy, comfortable process. It means letting go of preconceived ideas of order and human progress. Encountering the natural world is not principally about romps on the beach in the moonlight, but about *patient attention to connection, even where this leads to ambiguity and loss*. It means refusing to harmonize the horror by synthesizing it within a grander scheme. Adrienne Rich describes this patient attention as the ushering in of new visions of transcendence:

> But there comes a time – perhaps this is one of them –
> when we have to take ourselves more seriously or die;
> when we have to pull back from the incantations,
> rhythms we've moved to thoughtlessly,
> and disenthrall ourselves, bestow
> ourselves to silence, or a severer listening, cleansed
> of oratory, formulas, choruses, laments, static
> crowding the wires. We cut the wires,
> find ourselves in free-fall.[21]

Those who survive to speak a new language, the poet says, will find a whole new poetry in the discovery of connection:

> Visions begin to happen in such a life
> as if a woman quietly walked away
> from the argument and jargon in a room
> and sitting down in the kitchen, began turning in her lap
> bits of yarn, calico and velvet scraps,
> laying them out absently on the scrubbed boards
> in the lamplight, with small rainbow coloured shells
> sent in cotton-wool from somewhere far away,
> and skeins of milkweed from the nearest meadow . . .
> Such a composition has nothing to do with eternity,
> the striving for greatness, brilliance –
> only with the musing of a mind
> one with her body . . .
> pulling the tenets together
> with no mere will to mastery,
> only care for the many-lived, unending
> forms in which she finds herself.[22]

Discovering the pattern that connects is being liberated from the urge to dominate, to be 'master' over all one surveys, to superimpose order. From the contemplation of the 'many-lived, unending forms' springs a new ethic of care, understood more as 'patient attention to' than as identified with the stereotypical mother-role, which is the focus of so many feminist debates. From this patient attention can emerge authentic religious language, as is shown by Annie Dillard in *Pilgrim at Tinker Creek*.[23] Here I am drawing close to the understanding of Christian revelation as epiphany of the interconnectedness of God and creation. *Pilgrim at Tinker Creek* is a feminist post-modern story of a woman dwelling at Tinker Creek. For me it shows how the specificity, strength and richness of a particular context can be deepened from the perspective of connectedness, rather than be seen to contradict it.

For Annie Dillard brings no a priori judgements to the experience. Through simply being embedded in the situation, narrative, myth and ritual emerge. Truth and value are interwoven with the description of the moods of nature and the seasons. The matrix of the experience is simply fidelity to Tinker Creek – 'I live here'. Any account of the sacred, of evil, of ambiguity is wrested from the struggle to find a language for events, and not vice versa. Meaning and value emerge from this narrative fidelity to the Creek, not by generalizing from particulars, but by being faithful to them. And so, in his illuminating article, Jim Cheney shows how a different kind of meaning emerges:

> Tinker Creek transforms, subsumes the concepts of grace and forgiveness – and God. The Creek forgives – by dissolving evils, transforming them into sycamore leaves. If this sounds odd, Annie Dillard suggests, we might wash ourselves in the waters of Tinker Creek, any creek, and muse on the traditional concept of God on some true dawn, some true morning in our lives![24]

The ambiguity of the natural processes is very clear. But Annie Dillard does not disguise horror, waste, decay, or terrifying fecundity with a falsely-imposed unity. In fact this is a story of awakening to otherness and difference, to strangeness, to 'terror and a beauty insoluble'. Yet it is a confrontation with otherness *based on a fidelity to connection*. Second, it is a story of solitude. Annie Dillard remains alone. In her 'connected aloneness' she brings the revelation for me that the so-called 'existential estrangement' so beloved of Sartre, Tillich and a range of contemporary philosophers, is actually based on an estrangement of the 'disengaged I'. *The 'connected self' knows no existential estrangement*. 'Doubt not for whom the bell tolls', as Donne said, 'It tolls for thee', as we locate ourselves within the cycle of birth and death. (This is in no way to understress the problem of loneliness caused by the rejection of relation and connectedness.) This means that the whole Christian tradition of being in exile from the Garden of Eden, of a loss of connection with a creation, is not in fact the whole story of Christianity. Can we re-connect with a tradition which remained closer to the natural world? A tradition which, despite the dominant categories of distance and separation, is not overwhelmed with nostalgia to get back to the Garden, because *it never lost total contact with it*?

In order to tackle this question, another building block is necessary. I will now weave a further strand into this web of connection – albeit a somewhat tangled one. I want to see whether our metaphor can inspire a different way of coming to know the world and whether this will inspire another interpretation of Christian revelation. To do this I follow Perceval on the next step of his quest. Is he any closer to finding the right question?

6 Revelation and Connected Knowing

Twas about the dead of night,
And Athens lay in slumber;
Moonlight on the temples slept,
And touched the rocks with umber.
and the court of Mars were met
in grace and reverend number.

Evermore and evermore, Christians sing Alleluya.

Met they were to hear and judge
The teaching of a stranger.
O'er the ocean he had come,
Through want and toil and danger . . .

Athens heard and scorned it then,
Now Europe hath received it,
Wise men mocked and jeered it once,
Now children have believed it . . .

Evermore and evermore . . .

('Athens', *The Oxford Book of Carols*)

INTRODUCTION: THE HOLY FOOL AND THE CONFLICTING WISDOMS

The scene has shifted southwards to the craggy mountains of Greece. We become acutely aware of a beauty of sharp contrasts, mountains which seem dark and menacing, at the same time brooding over the tiny villages they overshadow with an almost primeval tenderness. We are within the ruins of the ancient Temple of Apollo at Delphi. The occasion is an International Congress on the Environment: it was thought that the beauty of the amphitheatre at Delphi should provoke the delegates to far-reaching decisions. With the snowy heights of Mount Parnassus behind, and the shining waters of the Gulf of Corinth in front, there could hardly have been a more inspirational setting. Yet already disquieting observations

81

were being made. It was clear that a small town like Delphi found great difficulty in coping with such a large assembly – in fact a new hotel had had to be constructed and many of the other guesthouses available for less important dignitaries had failed to come up to the required standards. The food was felt to be inadequate. As for an open-air gathering, without the protection of air-conditioning, several delegates had already decided to amuse themselves quite differently!

Logos was spared any of this discomfort. He had spent the night in Athens and was in excellent spirits. In fact, he had availed himself of there being a full moon and walked on the Acropolis at midnight. From its heights he had gazed over the city. There he had exulted in the tradition which the West had inherited from the wisdom of Greece and had handed on in such a sophisticated manner. He felt that his arguments and the tradition he stood for would attain their full force by being seen to stand in continuity with the ideas of Plato and Aristotle. Despite the enormity of the environmental crisis, there was nothing that reasoned analysis could not solve. In a mood of great confidence he boarded his executive helicopter for Delphi.

Perceval, too, had arrived at Delphi, but thoroughly weary and dispirited. He felt no nearer to finding the solutions he sought. He was confused as to why his quest had brought him in this direction: all he knew was that, wherever he journeyed, the earth which he loved was fast becoming a desolation. And now he saw that this woundedness threatened to be universal and permanent. Surely here, among the world's most famous scientists and politicians, there would be some ways forward? But the journey to Delphi had been disheartening. Whether he had hitch-hiked, or, more frequently, simply wandered through the countries of Europe, he was only too conscious of the interconnected suffering of people and land. The recent political freedom which many of these countries had experienced seemed to have brought little hope for the environment. What is more, the setting here in Delphi felt alien to Perceval. He was outside his own story, here amid the echoes of ancient gods and goddesses. He recalled how alien St Paul had felt in Athens and when he had been forced to confront the Temple of Diana at Ephesus. He wondered what kind of wisdom could emerge in such a pagan setting.

82

The splendour which accompanied the opening of the Congress left no room for complaints. It was a combination of the historic pageantry of the Olympic Games, the coronation of a monarch, and the opening of a State Parliament. Only the Holy Fool felt alien.

Logos sat excitedly awaiting his turn to give the key-note lecture. He felt the strength of his case would be overwhelming. But he accepted the fact that the first speech should be given by a Greek expert. To his surprise this turned out to be a woman – a Professor of Environmental Studies from the University of Athens. He prepared himself to be bored: no doubt there would be some sentimental plea to save a few dying species, recycle various trivial articles, save energy by wearing more pullovers in winter, avoid cancer by eating raw vegetables . . . And so on . . . . He had heard it all before and he knew that the solution did not lie at these levels.

To his surprise the Greek professor did not appeal to the emotions, or excite passions against the culling of baby seals. She appealed to *reason*. Logos could not believe it. Was this simply feeling (or intuition) heavily disguised? What is more, she claimed to have discovered an understanding of reason rooted in the history of the western tradition which, brought to the surface, promised to heal the wounds of the suffering earth. Logos, secure in the knowledge that his own solutions claimed the pedigree of Aristotelian logic, felt irritated and wrong-footed. She had stolen his own ground. If he had not known that he would have been branded as sexist, he would have stood up and contradicted the professor.

'I recall you to a different way of knowing', challenged the speaker, 'one which has been present to our tradition, but submerged in the dominant logic of control and domination. It is rooted in the wisdom of Ancient Greece through the wisdom of no less a person than Socrates! He it was who spoke of being a "midwife" to the thinking process. We do not own and control ideas, is what he meant – we nurture them to birth. And when they are born we do not own them. I challenge you to rediscover "connected knowing", which refuses separation between knower and known, bodily feeling from detached logic, and, crucially for us here today, which reveals the myriad connections with the hidden wisdoms of the natural world, our mutual interdependence.' She proceeded to image the difference which connected knowing would make: it would not be merely the technical solutions of problems, but rather a transformed manner of mutually coexisting with the whole of creation.

And then Perceval recognized the speaker. It was Sophia. In her he saw the wisdom of the Wise Woman so often despised or marginalized by warrior cultures. No longer did he feel threatened by the 'pagan' heritage of ancient Greece. Now he realized that the wisdom he sought at the end of his quest for the Holy Grail, which for him was incarnate in the Christian story, was the same search which now empowered Sophia in the face of the arrogance of Logos. In her he saw Cassandra, whose wisdom was doomed never to be listened to. In Sophia, too, the wisdom of the Pythian priestess of Apollo herself was rekindled – the priestess who spoke in riddles.

In Perceval's moment of revelation, one thing became clear. He had found his question. It was as crystal clear as the water from the Chalice Well at Glastonbury. *In the hearing into speech of the forgotten wisdom of connected knowing would lie the healing of the land.* The wisdom of connected knowing would challenge the logic which allowed the exploitation of the earth. But how, he wondered, would Logos ever listen to a different myth, another logic – that of Sophia? And how could culture begin to live by a myth different to the one which dooms creation to a slow dying?

The first step would be to step back into his own story, the Christian quest, and see it with new eyes.

KNOWING OUR WORLD, HEARING OUR STORY ANEW

In order to experience revelation as epiphanies of connection more awareness is needed of the ways through which we come to know self and world. In other words, we need consciousness raised on an epistemological level. This chapter seeks to uncover a more 'connected' way of knowing and to show its significance for the receiving of revelation. What was explored in the last chapter in terms of new relational understanding of the human subject is pushed further in terms of metaphors of knowing. Already this book has linked 'received knowing' with understanding revelation as the handing on of a body of doctrine – 'revealed truth' – from age to age. I have suggested that this is a very static notion of both tradition and revelation, frequently insensitive to context, language and culture, and excluding the experience of vast numbers of believers. Intuitive knowing was then seen as a way forward – an initial attempt to integrate knowledge of mind and heart – but lacking the means of linking individual experience with the communal and historical. The next step was seen to be 'procedural knowledge', which focused on the correct steps of the argument, yet was detached from the content of the decision. I now suggest that the way towards understanding God's revelation in a fuller and more inclusive manner is through what I call 'connected knowing'.

The insight offered by Sophia from the arena at Delphi is the cry from many contemporary cultures in different parts of the world. Since protest, march and revolution against a vast spectrum of injustices are failing to provide the mechanisms necessary for lasting structural change – so that millions of human beings have a chance of survival – it is time to restructure at the most basic level of consciousness. And what more basic than the way we come to know, perceive and feel? If we could become aware of the root metaphors or the mirrors through which, in a western culture, we understand ourselves, our relationships and our politico-social structures,[1] by tracking these to their roots, we become aware that our consciousness has been damaged at its very source. *Eradicating the roots of oppression in society and religion means changing these metaphors.*

Transforming the process of coming to know gives us new eyes for reading the sacred texts. How we read these texts, how we transmit tradition, is influenced to a great extent by our position in the world – our genderedness, race, societal status, sexual preference, health, and so on. These factors all form part of the process of our coming to know, of the basic experience of 'feeling the world', 'letting the world in'. This is what Alfred North Whitehead, in the language of process thought called 'prehension'. He described prehension as a flow of feeling from one subject to another.[2]

'Feeling the world', 'letting the world in' is a thoroughly

85

embodied process. We encounter the world and know each other as embodied beings. In all our acts of perception which ground the knowing process we are composed of feeling/ experiencing/hearing/touching/knowing processes of many selves.[3] As Catherine Keller wrote:

> Through my bodiliness I come to the animating knowledge that the energy of matter and the energy of soul are at base indistinguishable. Soul *matters*.[4]

'Animating knowledge', or connected knowing, recognizes this indistinguishability of the energy of bodiliness and soulfulness. It refuses to separate into the extremes of a 'nothing but' position ('We are all body/all mind/all soul'). Jung understood the psyche as inseparable from 'world'. He describes the symbols of the self as arising in the depths of the body: they express the self's materiality as much as the perceiving consciousness: 'At bottom the psyche is simply world'.[5]

The more archaic and 'deeper' the symbol is, the more *material*. The ecological thinking of the last ten years has awoken us to the part which the materiality of our natural surroundings plays in the formation of the psyche-self. It is not simply that the quality of diet, the purity of the air, the access to tree, plant and a variety of living creatures, form the material part of who we are. ('Man is what he eats', as we all know.) It is the quality of the way we relate and connect with this matrix, and the 'material' received for the process of 'soulmaking'.[6] The most significant development in contemporary theology is the promise which the ecological paradigm offers, as opposed to the hierarchical, dualistic one which has dominated tradition. This is what Anne Primavesi traced in her illuminating study referred to in chapter 4.[7]

From the area of pastoral practice the American Professor of Psychology, Howard Clinebell, shows how relationship with nature is now a vital – and hitherto ignored – factor in the pastoral therapeutic process.[8] One cannot be engaged with the healing and whole-ing of the self without being engaged with the healing of the planet. *Damage to the environment is also damage to the psyche at its most vulnerable level*. The wounded child is not only the hidden sufferings of childhood, of abused children, of the lost playfulness of the adult: it is also the child whose growth processes are stunted by inadequate food and polluted water; for whom 'nature' is no nurturing mother but terrifying and strange, to be escaped from through the seductions of technology.

So the first element in a 'connected' way of knowing is to link knowing with an attitude of Care. This has been described as 'caring knowing', 'maternal knowing' (Sara Ruddick), 'passionate knowing' (*Women's Ways of Knowing*), and 'empathic knowing'.[9] These are all different ways of trying to integrate the different voices and messages which we receive from our 'with-ness' to the world within a structural integrity. But this structural integrity is itself permeated by the rhythms of caring. Can we ever move away from downgrading 'Care' by viewing her through our individualistic lens, as a 'virtue' to be practised by benevolent individuals – particularly when our 'caring society' is blind to the predicament of enormous numbers of marginalized people? One way to begin is to listen to Heidegger's Myth of Care:

> Once when Care was crossing a river, she saw some clay; she thoughtfully took up a piece and began to shape it. While she was meditating on what she had made, Jupiter came by. 'Care' asked him to give it spirit, and this he gladly granted. But when she wanted her name to be bestowed upon it, he forbade this, and demanded that it be given his name instead. While 'Care' and Jupiter were disputing, Earth rose and desired that her own name be conferred on the creature, since she had furnished it with parts of her body. They asked Saturn to be their arbiter, and he made the following decision, which seemed a just one: 'Since you, Jupiter, have given it Spirit, you shall receive that Spirit at its death; and since you, Earth, have given it body, you shall receive its body. But since 'Care' first shaped this creature, she shall possess it as long as she lives. And because there is now a dispute among you as to its name, let it be called 'homo', for it is made out of *humus*, (earth).[10]

In this fable – Greek in origin – Heidegger is showing us that care is rooted in the basic dynamism and energies of growth. It is not to be confused with altruism or benevolence, or even Christian agape – at least according to the way Anders Nygren understands the agape/eros split.[11] Care is the energy of

87

paying attention to the 'many-lived, unending forms' referred
to in Adrienne Rich's poem (cited in chapter 4). But the ethics
of care to which I was referring spring from a knowing which is
'tending' and 'attending', cherishing, nourishing the intercon-
necting organic links between all living things. Care becomes
the basic dynamism of 'knowing' instead of the dynamism of
'control', detachment or objectivity. Sara Ruddick describes
the interconnection between attending and caring:

> This kind of attending was intimately concerned with caring;
> because I cared I re-read slowly, then I found myself watching
> more carefully, listening with patience, absorbed by gestures,
> moods and thoughts. The more I attended, the more deeply I
> cared. The domination of feeling by thought, which I had worked
> so hard to achieve, was breaking down.[12]

With caring knowing as a basic dynamism, it is possible to
tackle the roots of our confrontational logical patterns and
envision new possibilities.

Thus Andrea Nye's study *Words of Power* draws attention to
the dominant pattern of western logic as dualist, sexist and
intrinsically linked with the power discourse of the particular
political regime.[13] From Plato to Peter Abelard, from Abelard
to Locke, right through to the clear-cut demands of the
verificationists, western logic has developed as adversarial,
patriarchal and hierarchical. Being learned, being a scholar,
has been bound up with being able to destroy the position of
another. In ecclesiastical terms this has meant an over use of
Abelard's tool of *Sic et Non* ('Yes and No').[14] What does not
conform to the dominant model must be condemned as heresy.
The heretic is often he or she who refuses to fit into the linear,
hierarchical model of truth, who tries to stay with the contradictions, the ambiguities, the sheer messiness of the dialectics
of existence. The tragic irony, of course, is that Abelard died,
broken and a heretic, while his method lived on. The tragedy
of Abelard is that because the hierarchical system knew only a
vision of truth and logic which forced the dissenter or the weaker
to submission, the real relational truth of his own life was never
faced. The anguish of Héloise, wrote the Irish scholar, Helen
Waddell, to a friend, was to know herself in the end as unloved.
Caring knowing is not without its dimension of tragedy.

TOWARDS A LISTENING LOGIC

Connected knowing not only evokes a wider basis for knowledge than the disengaged rationalism of Locke and Descartes; not only does it attempt to hold together, to 'prehend' in Whitehead's terms, perception, feeling, emotion, sensation, ideas and images – in other words, the 'voices' arising from our being situated in the world; it also claims to be the fundamental meaning of logic itself. It is 'opposition', 'adversarial' or 'confrontational' logic which needs explanation and justification, not connected knowing. In a remarkable book, *The Other Side of Language: A Philosophy of Listening*, the Italian scholar Gemma Corradi Fiumara evokes a much fuller understanding of *logos*.[15] She recalls us to *logos'* derivation from the Greek verb *legein* which means far more than simply 'speech'. As Heidegger wrote:

> No-one would want to deny that in the language of the Greeks from early on 'legein' means to talk, to say or tell. However, just as early and even more originally, 'legein' means what is expressed in the similar German word 'legen': to lay down, to lay before. In 'legein' a bringing-together prevails, the Latin 'legere' understood as 'lesen', in the sense of collecting and bringing together. 'Legein' properly means the laying-down and laying-before which gathers itself and others.[16]

Moving on from this notion that knowing means 'a laying side by side', 'a letting-lie-together' within a sense of presence, the second important ingredient of logos is *listening*. It is a tragic aspect of current living that whereas we are bombarded in all directions with catastrophic prophecies about the planet, with pictures of human misery beyond our comprehension, we cannot 'hear' the truth of what they tell us, let alone respond in any commensurate way. We have robbed logos of its listening function. We lack a fundamental openness without which communication cannot flow. As Gadamer wrote:

> . . . this openness exists ultimately not only for the person to whom one listens, but rather anyone who listens is fundamentally open. Without this kind of openness to one another there is no genuine human relationship. Belonging together always also means being able to listen to one another.[17]

It is undeniable that we are a 'logocentric' culture. Words, speech, propositions, legal formulations, acres of daily newspapers, immense forests of the printed word invade and dominate our daily scene. But this high level of cognitive awareness has masked the fact that we cannot operate on other levels. Logos has become for us a means of 'epistemic control', or epistemic prejudice, which 'prevents us from seeing any different logical tradition because it is believed that it cannot be "logical"'.[18] Another tradition may be 'primitive', 'intuitive', animistic, but not logical.

If we were to recognize the narrow interpretation of logos in which we are imprisoned, if we were to embark upon becoming a listening culture, we might, says Fiumara, unblock the creative resources which have been immobilized by traditional 'logical' education. We might begin to perceive the forgotten, vitalizing connections in the midst of the storms and waves of cultural coexistence. Listening will function as part of the effort whereby we seek to establish a relationship between our world and different worlds.

This involves us in shifting from a cult of speech and control through wordiness, to a cult of what Fiumara called 'maieutics', or 'midwife thinking' – which is similar to what Sara Ruddick calls 'maternal thinking'.[19] This – as Sophia from the Delphic arena asserted – has its roots in the ideas of Socrates. In the Dialogue with Theaetetus, Socrates challenges Theaetetus with the fact that he is a midwife who practises midwifery.[20] He refers to the painful process of bringing-ideas-to-birth as midwifery – which he says is the task of the true philosopher. But he also points out that midwife philosophers are the true matchmakers:

Socrates: Did you ever remark that midwives are also most cunning matchmakers, and have a thorough knowledge of what unions are likely to produce a brave brood?

Theaetetus: No, I cannot say that I knew it.

Socrates: Then let me tell you that this is their greatest pride, more than cutting the umbilical cord. And if you reflect, you will see that the same art which cultivates and gathers in the fruits of the earth, will be most likely to know in what soils the several plants or seeds should be

> deposited . . . the true midwife is also the true and only matchmaker.[21]

The point is that the matchmaker knows how the best unions will be made (or in my terms the 'rightful connections'). But they are only effective because they are first and foremost midwife philosophers, who are by profession committed to the birth of thought. The midwife philosopher operates through a 'listening logic': the point of the activity, says Fiumara, is to welcome the nascent thinking in the act of being born, before it is swallowed up by culture into a stifling conformity. Listening logic makes room for other ways of knowing, the freedom of other ways of viewing the world and interpreting reality.

This is exactly what feminist thinkers have been stressing, in placing a high importance on 'hearing into speech',[22] and the primacy of metaphors of hearing over seeing. Whereas listening has been accepted as a tool of liberation theology, as a means of giving marginalized groups access to discourse, Plato shows us that listening, intuiting another logic, is actually the very heart of the whole process of reasoning. Where a listening culture is absent, what other alternative is there but to fall into the adversarial logic of Yes or No? When such a logic is controlled by those who hold the reins of power, small wonder that the logic of domination seems inevitable and decreed by 'the nature of things'.

Listening is an activity which requires the whole person. It requires the vulnerability to the other which is presupposed in the idea of the connected self.

In the context of the truths of faith, and revealed doctrine, a listening logic highlights the very fragility of these doctrines, dependent as they are on all the 'positional' factors mentioned earlier. Being vulnerable to each other allows 'other ways of knowing' their full space. What is more, it allows the shock of what Chung Hyun Kyung calls the 'epistemology of the broken body' to reach western consciousness:

> Pain and suffering are the epistemological starting point for Asian women in their search for the meaning of full humanity. The Asian woman knows the depth of humanity and the aching hearts of other women because she has suffered and lived in pain.[23]

An epistemology of the broken body, the way in which Asian women come to understand their selfhood and world of exploitation, is striking in its very otherness from the epistemology which emerges from privileged situations: *within a feminist praxis of liberation* it should spark off in western theology not only a 'metanoia' of listening, but a praxis of turning away from the past and a transformation of the future. Above all, this epistemological instability reveals to us the sheer vulnerability of God to our conceptual inadequacies.

Starting from the vulnerability of God and the 'humility' of being created – a humility based on 'humus', our earth-bound nature – does not mean espousing the doctrinal relativism popular today, despite what has been said about positional thinking. It is not just a question of black theology versus liberation theology versus traditional theology versus feminist theology versus fundamentalism (and so on), although it is vital to be aware of the position from which one reads the tradition. Nor is it a question of 'living only by a story' (see Don Cupitt)[24] with the two hidden assumptions that one story is as good as another, and that one gives up on theology in favour of ethics, including, of course, anything deserving of the name 'ultimate reality'.

I am arguing that the controversy over 'eternal truths of revelation' is deadlocked, first, because the underlying relation between truth and power structures is disguised; second, because theological doctrines are enunciated within a framework giving support to disengaged individualism and, third, that they are underpinned by a narrow, confrontational logic. It will be clear that I have been arguing for the inclusion of women, and drawing attention to 'sacrificed subjectivity', not solely because of injustice against women but because of the impoverishment of the entire system we have inherited and the way that distortions of theology underpin injustice in society. As always, the poorest and most marginalized of the world will carry on suffering this to an extreme degree.

Unless it could be different. Unless we dared to put flesh on the bones of the dream. Unless understanding God's communication in terms of 'epiphanies of connection' offers not just a vision of hope but possibilities for a different praxis. The journey starts here . . .

7 The Fragility of Divine Communication

> Authentic faithfulness to Tradition is creative and requires each generation to respond to new needs and challenges according to the dynamic of Tradition . . .
>
> Tradition carries an energy, a yeast that never stops causing the heavy dough of institutions to rise. From it springs an eternally new event, an ever new and ever to be renewed, meeting of each believer, in communion with all the rest . . .
>
> Sometimes Tradition even seems frozen under a great ice shell but below this frozen and rigid surface flow ever fresh springtime waters. It is up to us, with the help of God's grace, to break the ice that is above all the ice of our hearts become cold . . . From the ancient spring we will drink water that will give us new force so as to answer the questions of today.
>
> (Elizabeth Behr-Sigel, *The Ministry of Women in the Church*)[1]

A turning-point has been reached. It is time to see whether, with new eyes for reading (and ears for hearing), we can receive our heritage any differently. This chapter first asks what attitude we could have towards tradition. Is it contradicting the most precious feminist commitment to global justice to carry on, bent double as we are, under tradition's oppressive burden?

I then attempt to discover a liberating method of dealing with this tradition, and an image of the Godhead which will help us to move creatively onwards.

TRADITION - ORGANICALLY RE-IMAGED

Two questions must be answered. Why do Christian feminist liberation theologians remain wrestling with a tradition which is so clearly androcentric if not misogynist? Why not follow Mary Daly into the cosmic covenant of sisterhood and discover 'New Being'? Or admit, as Daphne Hampson does, that there is no way of redeeming a sexist past?[2] For indeed, no amount of re-imaging can escape the fact that Christian tradition presents us with a God symbolized as male, a male saviour arguably legitimizing a predominantly-male priesthood, and a Church which has condemned sexism as sin, but continues to exclude women from positions of authority. And consequent on this, why cling to Christian revelation? At a time when women are rediscovering Goddess traditions as powerful resources for rebuilding damaged self-esteem, why reclaim those sacrificial symbols which have had such fateful consequences for us?

In the first place I think we have to call the bluff of those who tell us that tradition is rigid and immobile – like the iceberg which Elizabeth Behr-Sigel so graphically describes above. As Anne-Louise Gilligan and Katherine Zappone assert in a recent article in the *Irish Times*, tradition can change exactly when the men in power want it to change![3] Can we focus our imaginations more creatively and hopefully on the flowing waters beneath, instead of the chilly peaks which immobilize us?

Second, the whole point of faith in God is at heart an experience of the dimension of ultimacy, of quest for depth of meaning, of the witness to a great love which enfolds all experience, human and non-human, a loving presence which has been experienced within a historical continuum. Human identity is constructed historically, and through a community's experience of faith and cultural history. Scarred and mutilated though our testimony to and representation of the divine may be, this intuition of ultimacy – to which the life of faith is response – permeates the language, the communal memory and the Christian symbol system. The same is true of every distinct cultural and religious group – which is why religious intolerance is so destructive of basic human identity. This does not mean that we are forced to carry 'the tradition' with us in the search for peace and justice, like an enormous furniture van forever dogging our footsteps, insisting on the use of the same heavy mahogany furniture for a spontaneous summer picnic! Rather, as I said earlier, we seek the nurturing, sustaining memories of divine presence and liberating action in the past to energize us in the present. The memory of the biblical Miriam's initiative has been a frequent inspiration for women from both south and north in reclaiming a usable tradition.[4] I

have tried to capture this sense of empowering memory
poetically by bringing Miriam into present-day Britain.
Miriam has been claimed as a prophetic figure in the current
struggle for leadership in the Christian Church. She has also
been painted by Lucy de Souza on the Indian 'Hunger Cloth',
commissioned by the German charity Misereor, as leading
her sisters in a dance of celebration of the gift of water in
a drought situation. I image her here as empowering black
women in Britain against racism – not because I have any
right to speak for black women, but in solidarity with their
struggle.

REMEMBERING MIRIAM: THE DREAM WHICH LIBERATES

I am Miriam, tall and free;
No longer victim, slave of oppressor's violence;
No longer will my people's heart be crushed
by alien laws,
by labour, stripping off the shreds of being woman;
This is freedom's day –
Egypt is no more – Jerusalem lies ahead!
And I will lead my sisters in the dance,
Wind, not whip, will strike our hair,
The salty spray of these wild waves – not sweat –
glistening on our faces,
The taste of pride in our beginnings,
The hope of fertile land our destiny,
And the presence of our liberating God
empowering, energising, summoning us to freedom!

I am Miriam, but now no longer tall and free,
I am Miriam, outcast and rejected,
Because I spoke out, with Aaron, against the marriage of
my brother,
I am stricken as one dead, not human, and must dwell
beyond the gates, deemed not fit for human sight.
Yet I will not blot out my hour of freedom –
Tho' my body has been shamed,
Tho' I am again in Egypt, rejected now – thrice bitter! –
by my own people,
I will hold alive the power of the dream which liberates,

And tho' my sisters and my people may walk through
history,
Trampled by the Pharaohs of society,
forever kept outside the city's Gate,
Denied the Shalom of Plenty,
Yet that fierce memory of freedom's dance
Will yet prevail . . .

I am Miriam and it is Egypt once again –
Tho' Egypt's name is Babylon.
Once more the crushed refuse-heap of shame,
We know the taste of alien corn,
The bread of slavery which chokes our throats –
How strangled are our cries!
The blackness of my sisters is become a shame, not
strength –
Yet black the night of freedom's memory,
Black the night of our God's presence –
Precious the love she showered on Sion!
And from her tender presence
springs the hope –
Tho' Babylon's oppressors stifle pride of race –
That we are not abandoned;
That Shalom of freedom will be ours . . .
And tho' our spirits be half-crushed –
O, I will hold my heart in readiness.

I am Miriam, now bent and broken,
And it is Britain, brave new world!
Still outcast, rejected from Shalom of plenty,
Cursed for skin and origin.
Still waiting at the Heathrow barrier,
Still waiting at the doors of job-exchange,
Still waiting for a council flat . . .
And yet, you Pharaohs wielding reins of power,
in Bank, Cathedral, board,
Seeing truth as white and English,
Know not the God of Justice!

Remember, Miriam! Remember waves of freedom!
Stride out once more tall and free
And lead our people in the dance!
Stride proudly through the Channel ports,
More powerfully into work that liberates,
Lay hold of God's fierce exultation,

The wildness of her redeeming power,
Holding your broken heart wide open,
In the long wait for God's Shalom,
which is your passionate gift to all.[5]

The notion of tradition as nurturing and sustaining memory – in this case the liberating memory of Miriam – could empower a different praxis. Here I simply use the idea of reclaiming the past to empower the present. The richness of 'making the connections' as a methodology, is that we are able to resource ourselves in the past, to overcome existential aloneness by connecting with community memory – where this is memory of liberation-in-action and truth-in-action. Hence a selection process is necessary and thus a hermeneutic of suspicion with regard to a rigidly-frozen canon of tradition. There are texts that cannot be proclaimed as liberating (for example, the story of the murdered concubine in Judges 19, referred to in chapter 2).

So reclaiming Miriam is but one example. But it is not simply a question of isolating individual figures who function as our personal inspiration. We also set free the frozen waters of a rigid tradition:

● By making clear from what context and within what community we ask our questions: for example, as I described in chapter 1, Hagar is of particular significance to women who, like her, are triply oppressed through racism, sexism and poverty. Thus a range of biblical women will have differing significance and liberating potential for diverse groups of women (and men) as their own suffering and oppression reaches articulation and analysis.

● By not isolating the person/group from the context and community, thus understanding the complex interactions of different oppressions, and how people reduced to degradation are forced to act with manipulative models of power. (For example, the only way Queen Esther could liberate her people was by playing up to patriarchal expectations of female charm.)

● By enlarging the meaning of 'text' to include symbol, art, music and popular forms of religion, thus discovering new revelatory meaning. For example, the three Synoptic Gospels agree in their story of the Garden of Gethsemane, where the apostles slept while Jesus prayed. Yet Fra Angelico, the Franciscan painter of San Marco, Florence, depicts Martha and the women watching and praying outside the Garden Gate. Another buried strand of the so-called rigid iceberg.

● Lastly, by exploring and discovering how communities of women have in fact been bearers of revelation through the ages, and have responded to the revelatory impulse – expressed in vision, dream, inspiration, insight – in unique ways. Clearly, the communities inspired by Hildegarde of Bingen and the Rhineland mystics, the communities of Béguines, the great Saxon Abbesses in Britain and Germany are of great significance. In fact the origins of most women's congregations are linked with a direct inspiration of the foundress. Usually a counter-cultural spirituality resulted, for example, with Mary Ward, foundress of the Institute of the Blessed Virgin Mary.

But what inspires confidence that the doctrines which have become essential to Christianity should forever be regarded as divine revelation? How can a prism of connectedness make any difference to the way these doctrines are received as revelation? First, Christianity witnesses above all to a God of love who freely chose to be manifest in history and human experience. The history of religious experience is of women, men and children startled by an experience of 'holiness of being' to which they give the name 'God'. Further, the ground of this experience is a response to something given – before all human attempts to grasp for it. *It is a profound sense of entering into a relation within which all life is response.*

The prism of connection is saying that this matrix of Being, the Creative Love at the heart of the universe, has been predominantly symbolized in a dualistic way, influenced by the logic of separation, in opposition to all that is human and limited. Further, where God is indeed depicted with human epithets, this is almost in exclusively masculine terms.[6] The apparent unworthiness of women to image the divine results in a dishonouring of the many-layered richness of creation. (We have not even begun to speak about the non-human representatives of divine creation.) Thus our experience of the divine permeating existence has been severely atrophied.

A metaphysic of connection sees the doctrine of God as Trinity, not in anthropomorphic terms as three males (or two and the Holy Spirit as female, which often results in a demoting of the role of the Spirit),[7] but as an attempt to image a God in movement, in process, a God whose whole being is to be in relation, to be relationality's core:

> This is the God who is urging us on to deepen our connectedness, weave new connections, unravel and re-weave the patterns of relating. The mystery of God's own becoming enfolds and unfolds as we move to new levels of relating and interdependencies.[8]

When we loose the Trinity from its sexist moorings, Marjorie Suchocki wrote,

> trinitarian thought should force us beyond our usual human categories, asking us to intuit a manyness in unity far beyond our experience, yet communicated to us in the deepest reality of communal justice.[9]

The incarnation of Jesus then becomes understood as the expression and tangibility of love making new connections, opening up new possibilities for justice-making. Matthew Fox evocatively expresses what happens in the man Jesus of Nazareth as the divine pattern of connectivity setting up its tent among us:[10]

> Jesus offered connections to the dispossessed in particular: to the lepers, women, slaves, sinners, and outcasts of society. He connects with them not only by conversations and scandalous associations at meals, but by undergoing the death of the unconnected, the death of the dispossessed at Golgotha'.[11]

I am increasingly convinced that the meaning of incarnation is so profound that we wilfully restrict it by seeing it totally encapsulated in the story of Jesus of Nazareth. What is revealed is relational power, the power of connection, which is of its essence not the private possession of an individual – as Jesus was well aware.[12] The very force of trinitarian faith is such as to teach us that the desire of God – truly the creative eros of God – to awaken us to the beauty and organic harmony of creation did not stop with Jesus, but is ceaselessly bringing to birth new possibilities for the universe, constantly weaving new connections. This is expressed by the doctrine of the Spirit of God as the energy of connection.[13] (I will develop this in chapter 8.)

The big difficulty which connection theology has to face is the following: If God is at home in the whole of the universe, revealing its intrinsic patterns of connectedness as harmonious, wholesome, and oriented towards the well-being of all living organisms, why do we imagine our eternal destiny as outside the universe? Why do we build churches as sacred places as a contrast – a 'condensing of the sacred' – to the world outside, if creation itself is the locus of the sacred?

The problem of the naming of good and evil is even more problematic: grappling with it involves facing the basic objection to a metaphysic of connection. For if God is seen as the source and resource of all the harmonious, interdependent systems and organisms which form the universe, ever 'luring' or energizing us to the creative realization of justice for the earth's inhabitants, how does evil, tragedy, injustice and loss fit into the picture? In solving the problem, are we not tempted back into a dualistic tension between good and evil, and thus the very dynamic which a metaphysic of connection is trying to replace? The following two chapters tackle these questions: How does God, imaged as source of connectedness, solve the problem of suffering, tragedy and evil (chapter 8)? Can there be a renewed understanding of Church within a metaphysic of connection and a non-dualistic theology of creation (chapter 9)?

8 God and Evil within a Metaphysic of Connection[1]

> Come, behold the works of the Lord,
> how he has wrought desolations in the earth.
> He breaks the bow and shatters the spear,
> He burns the chariots with fire!
> Be still and know that I am God.
> (Ps. 46.8–9)

> My heart recoils within me,
> My compassion grows warm and tender.
> I will not execute my fierce anger,
> I will not again destroy Ephraim;
> For I am God, not man,
> The Holy One in your midst,
> And I will not come to destroy.
> (Hosea 11.9)

> I am the Lord: I create weal and woe.
> (Isaiah 45.7)

Within the limits of a society which understood divine action primarily in terms of military intervention in its favour, the Jewish writers here struggle to enunciate another manner of the agency of God. The God of Psalm 46 is experienced as presence and stillness in the depths of the heart: not a stillness born of apathy or passivity, but one which drives to a different vision of the cosmos, a world operating without warfare. Hosea's vision is of a compassionate God, characterized by a fierce tenderness, specifically refusing to give vent to fury with violence: to act as God is to seek another way. Yet Isaiah introduces a completely different notion – the idea that God is somehow responsible for the creation of evil. This is something which Christianity has consistently rejected. The nearest it has got is with the suggestion that God somehow allows or permits evil to teach us – 'for our greater good', our full human development, and so on. So we are confronted with the problem of God in the face of evil as the greatest stumbling block to faith in a God of love. If a metaphysic of interconnectedness concentrates only on 'epiphanies of inter-connection' and harmony amid the many tragedies and suffering of earth and people alike, then it is no more use than any of the traditional theodicies offered to us to help us cope in this 'vale of tears'. As Ivan Karamazov cried (in Dostoevsky's *The Brothers Karamazov*), harmony is bought at an unacceptable price:

> And if the sufferings of children go to swell the sum of sufferings which was necessary to pay for the truth, then I protest that the truth is not worth such a price. I don't want HARMONY; and it's beyond our means to pay so much to enter on it. And so I hasten to give back my entrance-ticket; and if I am an honest man I am bound to give it back as soon as possible. It's not God that I don't accept, Alyosha, only I most respectfully return him the ticket.[2]

Nor is the contradiction between a God of love and a God who is all-powerful grappled with only in Christianity. (The dilemma is expressed thus: either God can but won't eradicate evil, in which case he cannot be good; or God cannot and therefore is not all-powerful.) How to cope with evil and suffering is the central issue for all religions, the reason why many people turn to religion, or, finding its resources fail them at the moment of crisis, have recourse to one of the many forms of atheism. As the famous Jewish novelist, Eli Wiesel cried, putting God on trial,

> He is Almighty, isn't He? He could use His might to save the victims, but He doesn't. On whose side is He? Could the killer kill without his blessing, without his complicity?[3]

In this chapter I attempt to show how the dilemma of evil and God is compounded by the oppositional understanding of good and evil, asking if the epistemological category of connected knowing (see chapter 5) within a metaphysic of connection can offer us a way through the situation. Does it help to understand how God acts in situations of suffering and tragedy? That will be the focus – not an exhaustive discussion of the many theodicies, or the different ways in which world faiths grapple with the problem. My underlying hope is, given the absence of women from the formation process of revelation (chapter 1), that women who have been scapegoated for sin in the course of Christian history, and victimized by its prevailing ethic of control and domination, may actually have insights to contribute to 'name us out of the depths' of the present impasse.

GENDER AND THEODICY

The gender-blindness with regard to theodicy (the justification of God in the face of evil) has masked the extent to which the whole theodicy problem is based on a dualistic oppositional framework of good and evil. By this I mean that 'good' is seen as absolute and unchanging, and achievable by the elimination of its opposite.[4] Because this framework gives rise to a set of damaging dualisms, according to which mind is superior to body, human to non-human nature, supernatural to natural, thought to feeling, some feminists have asked if the good/evil dichotomy is one which feminists should reject.[5] For women will always appear on the 'evil' side of the equation, it is said, and therefore sexism will always underpin the good/evil ideology. But if the absolutized dichotomy was challenged, would this remove the sexism and thus the accompanying scapegoating of women for evil?

This absolutized dichotomy between good and evil underlies all traditional theodicy attempts: the classical Hindu denial of the reality of evil, which is understood as 'maya', or illusion; St Augustine's early interpretation of evil as *privatio boni*, or deprivation of the 'good' (a view found also in the writings of Julian of Norwich,[6] as well as his later and more famous Free Will defence. There is also a fourth type, which I call 'God the Pedagogue' theodicy. It is this latter which demands clarification, since it remains the most popular among believers and indeed continues to evoke a stream of books in popular spirituality. Among philosophers of religion it is expounded by John Hick and Richard Swinburne. In its simplest form this theory asserts that suffering is the way God teaches us about life, the way we learn to become mature human beings and Christians. John Hick has his own refinement and claims continuity with the second-century Irenaeus of Lyons.[7] When we are born, he asserts, we live according to our biological possibilities (on the level of *bios*, or biological life); but in order to become God's creatures, to enter into a relationship of freedom and love with 'him', to live on the plane of *zoe* or human life, and attain our full potential, we have to learn through suffering. Suffering has a purpose here and is real and useful.

The powerful way this explanation has gripped our imaginations can be illustrated by C. S. Lewis's efforts to come to terms with his wife Joy's painful and tragic death:

> But is it credible that such extremities of torture should be necessary for us? Well, take your choice. The tortures occur. If they are unnecessary, there is no God or a bad one. If there is a good God, then these tortures are necessary. For no even moderately good Being could possibly inflict or permit them if they weren't.[8]

Feminist theology reacts strongly against such a justification of suffering. In the theology of creation which I am developing, to identify what is truly human as superior to the biological level is to downgrade the rest of creation. Hick also locates his theodicy in the next world. Our earthly life is a 'vale of soulmaking', and, although all appears a tragic failure in this life, eschatologically, all will be revealed and God justified. (How often have we heard this used as a means to make us put up with pain and injustice in the present? 'Another jewel in your crown in heaven!') The danger is that endurance of suffering is advocated instead of working for its eradication. Suffering is extolled as the means of becoming mature – as if delight, happiness, appreciation of beauty and so on could have no part in this. But the most harmful aspect of this theodicy is what it does to the concept of God. 'Who wants such a God?' cried Dorothee Soelle,

> Who gains anything from Him? Every explanation that looks away from the victim and identifies itself with a righteousness which is supposed to stand behind the suffering, has already taken a step in the direction of theological sadism, which wants to understand God as the torturer.[9]

It is a fundamentally human reaction to try to find a meaning to suffering which enables one to make sense and carry on living in the face of tragedy and horror. A feminist liberation theological analysis protests against the too-easily assigned meaning, the excusing of the horror in terms of assumed psychological growth. It is in the name of love and care for the name of God, and the well-being of the universe, that we protest and renounce such images of God as 'God the executioner', the God who punishes, tortures or educates through suffering. Such a God-concept has too long legitimized our human inflicting of pain on one another. If God can punish us by making us suffer – and Augustine understood the punishment of slavery and other injustices as punishment for the primeval sin of disobedience – then *the inflicting of pain becomes ethical*, because God is its prototype. We are seeing the tragic consequences of this theological sadism in the stories (still coming to light) of children being abused by their fathers. Rita Brock has argued powerfully in her article 'And a Little Child will lead us: Christology and Child Abuse' that God the Father sending Jesus to the cross is the prototype of child abuse, legitimizing it among human fathers.[10] Such an interpretation of cross theology may now be discredited,[11] but the link between divine punishment as ethical and patriarchal misuse of power remains indisputable. We must resist the temptation to give suffering 'meaning' too quickly. *Some* suffering can be redeemed – for example, through the lessons learned about life, or increased maturity – but *most* suffering is irredeemable. The murdered child, or the child who starved to death, remains the murdered or starved child, whatever consolation the stricken parents manage to discover. As I write, Morani Savaranamutti, the mother of a talented young actor and journalist in Sri Lanka who was murdered by the security troops, has returned to the country to lead the 'Mothers Front', which campaigns for an inquiry into clandestine killing. Her life is shattered, she cries, and nothing will bring him back. There is no possible meaning to assign to the atrocity. Yet she has adopted twenty-five children whose fathers have also been murdered.[12]

One of the most dishonest ways of coping with evil is not to name it in its stark reality. (I think of President Reagan naming the atomic bomb 'God's little Peace-maker'.) It is even more necessary to assert this at a time when new forms of racism emerge in Europe, in the wake of the unification of Germany and the new waves of refugees which recent political changes have caused. A generation which survived the Concentration Camp never imagined it would see the rise of neo-nazism. It was the gradual horror of what had happened in Auschwitz and Hiroshima, followed thirty years later by the genocide of the Vietnam War, which prompted the 'God is Dead' movement and laid bare the bankruptcy of the old theodicy models. Is it not better to admit the powerlessness and vulnerability of God than to believe in a God who allows such pain 'for our own good'? What possible 'good' is served by genocide?

Annie Dillard, sitting by Tinker Creek (see chapter 4), imposed no meaning on what she saw, including the savagery of nature, but allowed meaning – if any – to emerge from the situation. If it sounds too harsh that all suffering cannot be redeemed, this is not to say that it cannot be lived through and sustained. Perhaps we do not abolish evil but find a way through. This means that we have to reject all theodicies, or explanations of evil and suffering, which claim to offer final and total solutions, transforming all evil and suffering into everlasting harmony. And this because, first, they tend to excuse the mountain of injustice inflicted on people powerless to resist – as is the case of the Kurdish people in Iraq at present. Second, because they take no account of the 'dangerous memory of suffering' of many oppressed communities, which may be the only tangible form of divine presence. And third, because they distract from making right relation here and now.

How does a metaphysic of connection offer any better theodicy? Is it not a dishonest solution to offer a concept of God as nurturing and tender, source of dynamic connectedness, but powerless in the face of the real world? Surely the fact that the organic wholeness of creation in reality embraces so much that is catastrophic and savage, destroys any sense of ultimate beauty and harmony? If we maintain God as source of dynamic wholeness and then confront the broken connections which the world in fact manifests, the old classical dilemma still lurks, and God is not at all nice! As one feminist writer put it (in the context of a round-table discussion on the Goddess where the arguments are similar):

However certain one may be that one is loved by some presence in the universe – and it is possible at moments to be certain of that – that same presence will kill us all in turn, will visit our lovers with sudden devastating illness, will freeze our crops, will age our friends, and will never for one moment stand between us and any person who wishes us harm. Does the Goddess so care for us, if she is not moved by our pain? Does she nurture us when she blasts our fields with unrelenting sun? Did she, in some secret laboratory of vulnerable flesh, work out the mutations of the AIDS virus?[13]

These criticisms force us back to the question of whether God is responsible for evil. After all, the way all things interconnect can be destructive as well as healing. 'I create weal and woe', said the God of Isaiah. Is there not at least some ambiguity which should be introduced into a God concept? What kind of ambiguity? This I do with the idea of connected knowing: but first, I want to highlight the way in which women have been scapegoated for sin and evil and to show how this followed the logic of separation and the absolute confrontational dualism of good and evil I am trying to expose.

THE DEMONIZING OF THE FEMALE

Do you think that I have not read what the Fathers have said about women – since the beginning of the world? Do you think it is easy for a woman to read over and over again that she is a man's perdition? (Héloise, in *Peter Abelard* by Helen Waddell)[14]

The absolutizing of the good and evil polarity owes its grip on our consciousness partly to the successful association of women with responsibility for evil. Here, rather than repeating misogynist citations from the Fathers of the Church, I will show how this polarity manifests itself in the denigrating of the female body and its functions, through the supposed demonic forces at work in the female subconscious, and the scapegoating of women through myths of the fall – a fact frequently discussed by feminist theology.[15]

If good and evil are diametrically opposed, and the realm of the physical, sexual, bodily functions of reproducing, lactating, menstruating and excreting has been deemed inferior (by 'tradition') to the realm of pure spirit, it is easy to make women – more obviously associated with bodily rhythms – symbolize not only carnality, but demonized carnality. Fear and disgust at the female body has a clear history in both Judaism and Christianity – and beyond its boundaries up to the present day. Sartre, for example, identified the female body with holes and slime, found female sexuality obscene and the sex act the castration of man.

Within Christianity the effects of this opposition were that it became automatic to concentrate on sin as predominantly sexual, and for women to become scapegoated as sexual sinners – temptress, whore, the projection of the feared uncontrollable male lust. The iconography of Mary Magdalen as forgiven sexual sinner is a clear reminder of this; a woman who was clearly a disciple, who was commissioned to preach the resurrection, is nevertheless remembered as a prostitute.[16] The corollary of this is that the rejection of the female body becomes a form of sanctity: this is seen in the glorification of the Virgin Mary as *virgo intacta*, where bodily integrity is understood literally as a 'closed gate', which symbolizes a return to the state of primeval innocence. (Eve and Mary are frequently used as polar opposites – icons of the bad woman and the good woman.)

The demonization process works too at a subconscious level. When Jung produced his theory of personality types *animus* and *anima*, and identified specific masculine and feminine archetypal behaviour, it was not obvious that the same polarization underpinned his theory. 'This anima is so powerful', writes Demaris Wehr, that it upsets Jung's capacity to see real women. Whereas Sartre depicted female sexuality in terms of 'hole' on a biological level, Jung saw female sexuality on the level of the anima, the deepest level of personality:

> Finally it should be remarked that emptiness is a great feminine secret. It is something absolutely alien to man; the chasm, the unplumbed depths, the yin. The pitifulness of this vacuous nonentity goes to his heart (I speak here as a man), and one is tempted to say that this constitutes the whole mystery of women. Such a female is fate itself. A man may say what he likes about it; be for it or against it, or both at once, in the end he falls, absurdly happy, into this pit, or, if he doesn't, he has missed and bungled his only chance of making a man of himself.[17]

The sense of the otherness of women which comes to the fore so strongly in this passage is even more strongly expressed when describing the symbolism of the mother. Jung calls it a perilous image: the mother is the compensation for all the risks, struggles and sacrifices which the man must make; at the same time she is the great illusionist and seductress, who draws him into life's 'frightful paradoxes where good and evil, success and ruin, hope and despair counterbalance one another'.[18] This is the flip side of the coin of the (idealized) image of the tender, nurturing mother. In the image of the 'devouring mother' – think of the witch in *Hansel and Gretel* who prepared to eat the children – there is condensed the misogynistic fear of woman's body as 'the dark continent', and the terror of sexuality as uncontrollable, as opposed to pure reason and spirit. (The *Confessions* of St Augustine are an unparalleled testimony to this struggle.)[19]

Mozart's opera *The Magic Flute* contains a clear example of the demonization of the mother. The story is based on the mysteries of the Egyptian goddess Isis. The tension lies between the Queen of the Night – mother of the heroine, Pamina – and the Masonic brotherhood with its leader Sarastro. Where do good and evil lie? Our hero, Tamino, is initially confused. With the Queen of the Night or with Sarastro? A reversal takes place, by scapegoating the Queen of the Night as source of all hatred – and incidentally ruining the mother–daughter relationship in one fell swoop (which is a familiar motif in patriarchal mythology: it would appear that the Demeter–Persephone legend is the sole survivor of an undistorted mother–daughter relationship).[20] The point seems to be to ensure the succession of the brotherhood through the suppression of the dark (=female) forces.

How much hatred is contained in the 'devouring mother' stereotype is shown by the (Freudian) psychologist Ernst Becker, in a passage which makes clear that the vulnerability experienced by physicalness is then projected onto the mother as source:

> The real threat of the mother comes to be associated with her physicalness. Her genitals are used as a convenient focus for the child's obsession with the problem of physicalness. If the mother is a goddess of light, she is also a witch of the dark. He sees her tie

109

to the earth, her secret bodily processes that bind her to nature; the breast with its mysterious sticky milk, the menstrual odours and blood, the almost continual immersions of the productive mother in her corporeality, and not least . . . *the often neurotic and helpless character of this immersion.* . . . The mother must exude determinism and the child expresses his horror at his complete dependency on what is physically vulnerable . . . *he seems more 'symbolically free', represents the vast world outside the home, social world with its organized triumph over nature, the very escape from contingency which the child seeks* [my emphasis][21]

The fear of the limitations and messiness of the bodily processes could hardly be expressed more clearly. The (male) need to escape the 'world of the female' (bodily, irrational and particular), to enter the transcendent world beyond (spiritual, rational and universal) has already been discussed, but is seen here as the backdrop to the good/evil dichotomy.

If one challenges this dichotomy through the prism of connected knowing, what then?

CONNECTED KNOWING, AMBIGUITY AND GOD

Connected knowing emerges from a way of experiencing the world in all its complexity and ambiguity. It recognizes the interweaving of good and evil, of passion, pain and celebration in human living. It suggests that the chaotic, messy and irrational elements of living are swept under the carpet at the expense of understanding authentic wholeness. Connected knowing does not flee difficult alternatives by flight into false innocence (I wash my hands of this mess) or forcible control (send in the troops).

This way of knowing is steadfast in the face of the tragic dimension of life and open to the creative possibilities of new situations. It seeks to maintain a balance between the temptation (of the dominant group) to order and control, and the necessity for affective, compassionate response to form part of decision-making, and thus a different basis for ethics. Connected knowing means refusal to scapegoat one sex for the erotic feeling and bodily processes which contribute to the formation of ego-integrity for men and women. That which has been downgraded, despised or spiritualized away by

negative strands of Christian theology – namely body-wisdom
– has to be reclaimed as life-affirming energy. Thus we will
touch again 'the smiling vital force', the alternative beyond the
dualisms, to which Cassandra referred (see Intermezzo). We
will reach again the sense of sacredness of the earth and the
whole of creation, to which Scripture points but which a
destructive focus on humanity as Colossus bestriding creation
has obscured. Hopefully, women will no longer need to
symbolize a despised carnality which *homo spiritualis* must
shun. For instead of transcendence being seen as transcendence
of the physical, the sexual and the particular, it will be re-
imaged as *a liberating crossing-over, out of the limits of
separation into a richer and juster connection with people and with
all living things.*

This does not mean a lapse into paganism, a naive
withdrawal from politics into the arms of nature-goddesses,
exchanging reason for a few magic spells. Nor is it self-
indulgence or a blurring of moral sensitivity. Understanding
what Christianity deemed necessary to reject in the old
Goddess religions is an important exercise in itself: there are
valuable resources here being reclaimed by Goddess circles
and their absence has brought impoverishment to humanity.
Nor does it mean a rejection of what is (unhistorically) called
'the tradition'. It is a summons to understand this tradition not
as monolith, but an interacting web of traditions, a tapestry of
innumerable threads, in which one thread became dominant at
the expense of all the rest.

What it does mean is an invitation to re-connect and re-
integrate with rhythms we have lost – the recovery of herbal
lore and the development of solar energy are two examples of
this. The ethics of connection which result are a summons to
respect difference – the difference manifested by those
compelled to become minority groups in society (the life-style,
community traditions and values of North American Indians
and Australian aboriginals, to give examples) – as well as
difference between women, men and children themselves.[22] It
is a summons, more importantly, to commit ourselves to the
exploited other, by adopting different ethical priorities and by
realizing that we ourselves in the rich North are partly
responsible for the problems in the poor South.

Attempting to find meaning, and a means of living through tragedy, decay and loss has been the aim of all religious faiths since the beginning of time. The challenge is to discern which forms of suffering and evil belong to the natural cycle of birth/death/rebirth, and which are the result of human injustice and exploitation, with awareness of the considerable overlapping of the two areas.

By the 'ambiguity' of complex situations I do not mean that moral evil is at all ambiguous. The abuse of a child is not ambiguous. Nor were the death-camps of the Second World War, or the African famine. Suggesting that God is present to ambiguity might seem to imply God condoning the horror. I mean two things. First, there is a tragic element accompanying the processes of birth and death. We will never overcome finitude, or the necessity of death – our own and the loss of loved ones. This is where we do need to separate, but for the sake of making another sort of connection. When death comes to one who is 'old and full of years', despite the grief of loss, there can be a sense of completion, of the rightness of an earthly life coming to a close. But it is untimely death, agonizing death through accident, war, violence, abuse, starvation, poverty, or one of the diseases brought on by the excesses of life-style, which makes us call the conditions of dying for which we are responsible 'evil'. And thus we despair that life has any meaning.

Second, recognizing ambiguity means attempting to get beyond oppositional consciousness in an attempt to solve ethical problems. Connected knowing comes to terms with the complicated historical build-up to a difficult political situation (for example, the Gulf War, the Arab–Jewish conflict), or a moral dilemma (the abortion issue). We can never undo the history of imperialist warfare which is part of the background of the former, nor the entrenched interests which led to the polarization 'pro-choice' or 'pro-life' of the latter. But we can respond to the challenge to find a partial solution which respects the complexity of the issue, without falling into either 'false innocence' or the ethics of dominant control.

For 'innocence' in its Latin origin means not a passive non-involvement, but an active 'not injuring', not inflicting harm.[23] Within an epistemology of connection innocence is the attempt to create conditions for the resolution of conflicts amid the storms of conflicting interest and cultures. The Jesuit martyrs of El Salvador would be examples of this: the fragile peace in that war-torn country has been won at the cost of their lives, lives totally poured out in denunciation of an unjust war, not in fleeing from involvement. Connected knowing sees the human will – for Augustine, source of the primeval fall – as embedded in structures of care and connection. ('Care' is here seen not as individual virtue, but as an energy drawing us to make connection, to pay attention to relation.) Rooted in structures which respect both carer and cared-for, the human will becomes not a narrow, individualist self-will, pitted against another, but an integrative power, fuelling relational energy by its degree of attention to all facets of the person-in-relationship.

How, then, do we experience the activity of God meeting us in the experience of suffering? We do it by an insistence on the tragic dimension of life, on complexity, ambiguity and partial solutions. Is God thereby robbed of any sense of power in the face of suffering and evil? The God we call upon is far from the *deus-ex-machina* invoked by Greek tragedians – and modern pantomimes – to solve the crisis. To envision God as source or power-in-relation (Carter Heyward), right relation itself (Sharon Welch), Shalom of Being (Rosemary Ruether), source of redeeming connection (myself), the lure to realize new connections (Catherine Keller), or the power of compassion (Wendy Farley),[24] is first to redefine transcendence and immanence. Not only do we say farewell to the God of exclusion, the totally other, the controlling divine Parent, but *we do not see divine transcendence and immanence as sharply opposed polarities*. They are rather 'mutually enriching dimensions', as Grace Jantzen has explained.[25] On the basis of the connected self, immanence is not inert, static passivity, which must be activated from without, but a rich, many-layered interiority,[26] where the divine energizes our heart's desire, our passion for justice, our thirst for meaningful relating. Immanence is the delightful assurance that God is present to the particular, the concrete situation, with all the fullness which human beings can bear. (Alas, we cannot bear very much.)

The transcendence of God is the power which draws us to the relational heart of the universe. Transcendence asserts that

God takes the initiative in creating/redeeming activity. It is the guarantee against the overly-simplistic Feuerbachian reversal, 'Talk about God is merely talk about man'. Transcendence is the pledge that the anguish of a particular era, the suffering of an oppressed group is never forgotten, but held in the 'dark knowing of God', as 'dangerous memory', to be channelled into new redeeming possibilities.

This entails that the personhood of God is intimately bound up with the world's materiality. Most people, vaguely haunted by fears of pantheism, find it difficult, if the omnipotence, omniscience and unchangeability of God are removed, to face there being no ultimate refuge for human insecurity. They also find it difficult to see how God could be God in any convincing way. Associating the personhood of God with the decay of cruelty and savagery in nature would appear little short of blasphemy!

But Grace Jantzen in *God's World, God's Body*[27] presents a view which respects both God's immanent presence and transcendence. The world's wounds are God's wounds. God's body is vulnerable to the wounds we inflict on it – desertification in Africa and India, the Chernobyl disaster – and so we can speak of the death of God, tragedy in God. How then can we understand God's action in any meaningful way? *By trusting the promise of the model of revelation as the power of connectedness.* God's presence is a vulnerable presence, because the connections are fragile; goodness is fragile in a broken world.[28] Divine power works – but not as control or coercion. Rather, the power and energy of connectedness work, in situations of suffering, as the power of compassion.

GOD'S POWER AS THE POWER OF COMPASSION

We seek an alternative principle of empowerment in community rather than power over and disabling others. Such enabling in community is based on a recognition of the fundamental connectedness of life, of men and women, of blacks and whites, Americans and Nicaraguans, Americans and Russians, humans and the non-human community of animals, plants, air and water. Nobody wins unless all win.
(Rosemary Ruether)

114

Wendy Farley has developed a theodicy based on divine power as the power of compassion.[29] Compassion for her – similar to the way I redefined 'care' – is not a feeling but a relational mode, and a power. It includes the idea of 'sympathetic knowledge' of the other's suffering (connected knowing?), although she is aware that there is no way of identifying with another's experience.[30] Compassion is an enduring disposition, which integrates many dimensions into a coherent model of world-engagement, as the whole self becomes a servant of compassion's care for the world. Compassion is not a one-sided, paternalistic pity, but is a form of love, the disposition to love in a world filled with suffering; indeed, it is love in the encounter with suffering, always respecting the integrity of the other. Compassion is the power which drives to justice, beyond the narrow limits of a legalism which contents itself with punishing the wicked.[31] Compassion is an efficacy for transformation, an empowering power, and a power for preservation. Lastly, it is a 'power to bring to life what is broken by pain, to bring to justice and redemption what is twisted by brutality'.[32] Here is the germ of a solution to the apparent failure of God to end suffering. *The failure of compassion must be seen not as a failure of God, but a failure of human response. The innate relational character of compassion reveals God's vulnerability.* Power and vulnerability seem to be contradictions, yet we run away from the paradox with great loss.

How does this help the believer in situations of suffering? A believer, experiencing her own subjectivity, relationships and events in a faith context, wants to be energized by faith, not told that God is vengeful, dead or powerless. She seeks not so much a theodicy, but resources for coping with suffering, a way of seeing in the dark. She seeks deeper understanding of her own responsibility for the evil and suffering encountered in personal and communal situations, as well as the experience of divine compassionate presence at work within them, ceaselessly offering all that is possible for healing and whole-making in a given context.

Facing up to personal responsibility demands sensitivity to context, power relations, culture and community. It brings a different sense of accountability according to whether one is rich or poor, from the dominant white group or ethnically marginalized. 'Dangerous memory' as a tool for recalling God's power in situations of oppression works in different ways, according to whether one is oppressed or belongs to the group in power. Dangerous memory for the oppressed group, as Sharon Welch, following Jean-Baptist Metz, wrote, is 'the dangerous memory of freedom':

> This memory leads Christianity to a critique of what is commonly accepted as plausible; dangerous memory leads to political action. Dangerous memories fund a community's sense of dignity; they inspire and empower those who challenge oppression. Dangerous memories are a people's history of resistance and struggle, of dignity and transcendence in the face of oppression.[33]

Remembering how the compassionate God acted in the past as source of empowerment for the present is one sort of remembering. But for those who were actively engaged in the oppressing, there is a different sort of remembering. It could be called a 'metanoic' memory, a remembering which fearlessly and with humility 'makes the connections'. And the connections bring about metanoia or conversion. They bring the horror of realizing the dominant white group's responsibility for, for example, the slave trade, and the colonial, imperialistic movements which are the historical background to so much present misery. And women colluded in these movements.

Recognizing the way in which white women colluded in the exploitation, realizing that one will always be a 'recovering racist' – as Susan Thistlethwaite has said[34] – is one specific example of what revelation as 'the pattern which connects' means. No real connection or dialogue between exploiter and victim is possible without the former's commitment to ongoing conversion. Being able to stay with the memory – not so as to wallow in guilt feelings, but so as to take deeper responsibility for the present scene – is one important way of experiencing how God works in the face of evil.

EVIL: A GHASTLY MIMICRY OF THE ENERGIES OF JUST CONNECTION

The revelation which comes through the logic of listening and hearing into speech is a dawning awareness of the fragility of connection. God's compassionate presence, which is an energy driving to just connection, is revealed as the basic rhythm of creation. In contrast, sin and evil are the reverse energies: sin is structural de-creation, causing the ontological uncreating of the self, community, the breakdown of natural systems, the turning of energies into 'mutually assured destructiveness'. It is a ghastly mimicry of the process of creation described in Genesis, a blocking of the grain of existence (as was described in chapter 4, in the context of torture). In this sense one begins to understand what the mystics, both Christian and from many religious traditions, tell us about sin as 'nothing'. As Julian of Norwich wrote:

> But I did not see sin, for I believe that it has no kind of substance, no share in being, nor can it be recognised except by the pain caused by it.[35]

Clearly, neither Julian – nor Augustine who expressed the same view earlier[36] – meant that one should dismiss the world of evil and suffering as 'nothing'. But on an ontological level, if goodness consists in a correct vision, namely the vision of the harmony of the interdependence of all living things, then the dis-connectedness resulting from structural de-creation has no corresponding validity. Broken connections are no-thing. (C. S. Lewis was intuiting the same thing when, in *The Great Divorce*, he pictured sin and evil as grey and formless, whereas grace and goodness are 'weighty', fully-formed and radiant.)[37]

Structural evil – as was discussed in chapter 4 – expresses the structures of unmaking, a demonic reversal of the nurturing tenderness which called creation into being. Equally striking as torture as example of this is the activity of making war.[38] War is basically the activity of out-injuring the other person under the pretext of territorial claims, which often remain unchanged at the end of the assault. (For example, what power-relations have been changed after the Gulf War? Innocent people have been killed and terrible environmental damage inflicted, but the West remains locked in the same conflict with Saddam Hussein.) The speed of injuring is central and the feat of out-injuring determines the winner. False naming is also part of the process: codes, bluffing, mystification, camouflage and deceit are part and parcel of the grammar of war:

> The lies, fictions, falsifications within war, though authored by particular kinds of speakers in any given instance . . . themselves collectively objectify and extend the formal fact of what war is, the suspension of the reality of constructs, the systematic retraction of all benign forms of substance from the artefacts of civilisation, and, simultaneously, the mining of the ultimate substance, the ultimate source of substantiation, the extraction of the physical basis of reality from its dark hiding place in the body out into the light of day.[39]

The structures of de-creating have become an accepted part of the way we interact, as the logic of separation made clear. When the members of an ethnic group interfere with the process of the dominant group's gaining of control, they are denied physical needs, the possibility of community life, except of the most basic nature, in a way designed to make it difficult for them to survive (for example, the refugee camps). And, finally, they are denied a history, a culture and a tradition. (Iraqi troops dug up the bodies of Kurdish women shot down in the fields to make sure that no symbols of Kurdish identity were buried with them. Africans are forced to visit the museums of the colonizers in order to re-discover a lost heritage.)

The point is clear. But the analysis of societal evil as the structures of un-creating also sheds light on the question of God's presence and ambiguity. Because structural de-creation has acquired historical form within our institutions - and therefore a pseudo-authority - God-talk can become an ideology to give it credibility. The images of God the punisher, the executioner, the pedagogue (with which I began this chapter), present no challenge to the forces of structural un-making. So God becomes vulnerable to the way evil is defined by those in power.

But God is God and does not abandon us: 'I am God, not man . . .' as the prophet Hosea declared (Hosea 11.9). Rather, God's involvement attunes itself to the suffering which the structural un-making has caused - human beings ravaged by disease consequent on life-style and environmental degradation, alcoholism, drugs, sexual and racial abuse and poverty. Solutions are partial because limited by the personal and political resources available.

We need to name God in such a way that the structures of un-making are denounced. To do this we need to break out of the individualist situation (into which the structural de-creation forces us), relating our suffering to the group experience and to social analysis. For patriarchy is at its most successful when it makes women believe that they are alone in their suffering (of violence, isolation with small children, poverty, subordination and so on) and therefore guilty and ashamed. The first step in naming oneself out of the depths is to discover the communal nature of the suffering. This is as true for sufferers of abuse, of wasting diseases, alcoholism, people with AIDS, as it is for the systemic racism endemic in society. Even for the most marginalized groups there is a communal memory – of identity, freedom and hope – to provide resources. Remaining within the community's historical memory is to plug into the structures of creating, and to re-discover divine power at work in structural evil.

In order to do this we need spaces for community, dialogue and trust.

9   The Church: Permanently Marginal or Leaven for Change?

Liberation theology is a practical, communal, revolutionary type of ecclesia that is rooted in the Christian past and worthy of further implementation in the present and in the future. Liberation theology presents one with the choice to be part of the underground church, part of the Christianity that has been committed to liberation in history and to solidarity with the oppressed.
(Sharon Welch, *Communities of Resistance and Solidarity*)[1]

Dinner began with a ceremony of children. Jean-Marie carried the little clown-girl in his arms to show her the Christmas Tree and the Nativity stable and the sparks dancing from the big pine logs . . .
Then the feast began, ample, cheerful and noisy, with everyone primed on Anneliese's punch and fuelled with Rhine wine . . . . [Mr Atha] dipped a crust of bread in the wine and fed it to her [the child], morsel by morsel. As he did so, he talked, quietly and persuasively. 'I know what you are thinking. You need a sign. What better one could I give than to make this little one whole and new? I could do it; but I will not. I am the Lord and not a conjuror. I gave this mite a gift which I denied to all of you – eternal innocence. To you she looks imperfect – but to me she is flawless . . . She will never pervert or destroy the work of my Father's hands. . . . She will remind you every day that I am who I am, that my ways are not yours, and that the smallest dust mote whirled in darkest space does not fall out of my hand. I have chosen you. You have not chosen me. This little one is my sign to you. Treasure her!
(Morris West, *The Clowns of God*)[2]

These two quotations sum up the tensions of the present scene as regards the possibility for redeeming Christian community today. Working from a 'connection theology' it is clear that authentic community is the prerequisite both for the blossoming of the connected self as well as the recovery of healing connection in every area of society. Sharon Welch expresses the near despair resulting from identification with the oppressed: it is the desperation of being forever marginalized, of being an underground community, always in conflict with hierarchical misuse of power. Morris West (if one ignores some of the sexism in the novel, as well as the excluding male language) expresses the dilemma in a poignant way. For the little community gathered together to celebrate Christmas consists of a few outcasts from society – Judith, the hunchback, who painted the 'cosmos' cup, the Downs' syndrome child of the quotation, Mr Atha, the stroke-patient healer (and the Christ figure in the story), and of course Jean-Marie, the pope fleeing the Vatican because of his intuition of a coming nuclear holocaust. (It is a community in which Perceval would feel at home.) They are all 'Clowns of God', marginal to society, yet all having 'iconic' or revealing significance as to how God is active in times of crisis.

The dilemma which these quotations presents for a feminist liberation ecclesiology is the intuition of being forever relegated to marginal status. The dream of a common language, of the 'beloved community' rising phoenix-like from the ashes of patriarchy, seems but a deluding fantasy, a forlorn hope. Is marginal existence as a pressure group, or as a nurturing refuge from an unjust world, the most that can be hoped for for feminist ecclesiology?

This chapter attempts to show how the insights of a feminist ecclesiology are crucial for the very survival of Christian Church. The first step (from within a connection theology) is to show how the possibility for any community is linked with basic ecological factors. Second, I discuss three examples of hope-filled community emerging from feminist theology. Then I will show how a renewed theology of the Spirit is the fundamental characteristic of renewed community. This will be seen to prompt a reawakening of the prophetic and mystical dimensions of Church. And this may be God's unique revelation for our times.

BROKEN CONNECTION AND THE REDISCOVERY OF COMMUNITY

That the very possibility for human community is related to the connectedness of human beings with the environment's nurture was brought home to me powerfully on a visit to

Rajasthan, North India. The area most stricken by drought which we visited was the district of Rengi. Its problems are made more severe because any water which can be found is salty and unfit for drinking. The consequences for Rengi as a living possibility are disastrous. The land has turned to desert and whole villages are abandoned. At least, not quite. There are villages where women and children live alone, because the men have either abandoned them or gone in search of work. There are other villages where there can be no marriages – as families will not send their daughters to villages where there is no water. The very possibility of human community has been removed. There remains only isolation, disease and human desperation. The story of Rengi is one part of an enormous picture of the interweaving of environmental degradation and human suffering.

I will describe three different kinds of response towards creating just community, working from the perspective of feminist liberation theology, and then move to a theological analysis. The purpose is not to chronicle a history, or to make a comprehensive survey, but to bring to light factors contributing to a renewed ecclesiology. The hope is that the 'beloved community of the dream' so integral to feminist liberation theology will become neither marginal, nor a new centre of domination, but that *from the margins will flow a new centre* and the dismantling of patriarchy. This method is followed because what is needed for the realization of authentic community today is not only dream and vision, which is occurring in many places, but the envisioning of how to get from dream to reality, how to move from the intimate atmosphere of a group working from a consensus model of authority, to an organization which knows no way of conducting itself other than rigid authoritarianism.

The first sign of hope for authentic community offered here, one which from its origin in America is becoming a rising tide in many parts of the world, is the Women-Church movement,[3] the 'ecclesia of women'. I want to show how the three different forms in which this has been expressed so far are living witness that Church does not have to be oppressive or irrelevant, but can yet be the very leaven for change which the gospel proclaims. This is proof that, although tradition may appear to

122

be an immovable iceberg whose icy (visible) summit symbolizes its intransigent depths, this threatening iceberg can be broken up to allow the waters beneath to flow, change and transform.

Women-Church, born in Chicago, USA, in 1977, held its first large meeting in November 1983. Called 'From Generation to Generation: Woman-Church speaks', its primary declaration was that *Women are Church*. As Rosemary Ruether expressed it, 'This means women engaged in liberation from patriarchy declare this community of women's liberation to be theologically, church, that is to say, a community of redemption.'[4] This makes it clear – as I described in chapter 2 – that women are exiles not from the Church, but from patriarchy. What I there related as an Exodus movement to the wilderness, in response to unjust structures and the refusal to ordain women in the Church of England, can now be given an *ecclesial* dimension. For Ruether writes:

> As Women-Church we claim the authentic mission of Christ, the true mission of the Church, the real agenda of our Mother-Father God who comes to restore and not to destroy our humanity, who comes to ransom the captives and reclaim the earth as our Promised Land.[5]

'Exodus' for Women-Church means a deliberate leaving behind of oppressive and excluding patterns of being Church. It means the deliberate option of ministering to the needs of those whose needs are unmet by these excluding patterns. (The imagery of being in the wilderness has spoken evocatively both to the situation of women in institutional Church, as well as to those struggling to teach theology from a feminist perspective in colleges and universities.) What has to be stressed is that *women are not leavers*. Most women who work with Women-Church groups have one foot in and one foot out of the structures. Elisabeth Schüssler Fiorenza calls this an Insider–Outsider position. Riet Bons-Storm, Professor of Pastoral Theology in Groningen University, The Netherlands, calls it 'ministering to each other outside the Father's house'.[6] Fiorenza herself has described her vision of Women-Church as that of 'discipleship of equals'.[7] This is close to the image of ecclesia as 'healing the broken connections', the image which I am proposing. The discipleship of equals evokes a deeper level of community than the claiming of equal rights of liberal individualism – the level at which the ordination debate is frequently conducted. Fiorenza evokes mutuality-in-relating as the vision of the Jesus movement, which, through the centuries (she claims) has never been totally lost sight of.

More recently she has developed her understanding towards seeing Women-Church as a space which is open yet bounded, where the overlapping communities of women of different faiths, creeds, race and class can be in dialogue. This is in response to the changed consciousness in feminist theology which puts far more emphasis on the differences between women, rather than the sheer fact of femaleness as the overriding uniting factor. This image is important in drawing attention to the fact that women are in dialogue across the faith boundaries – a fact which can have important consequences for ecumenism at a time of apparent deadlock. For example, in the summer of 1991 in London, an initiative of the Inter-faith Network convened about sixty women from different faiths around the issue of health. The seminar was chaired by the Minister of Health, Mrs Virginia Bottomley, who was amazed that religion and faith networks had such uniting potential and strong, political articulation from women of such disparate backgrounds.

This points to an important aspect of Women-Church. Many people – including women – shrink from the term as 'too churchy', as preserving the very characteristics of Church from which they wish to escape. Even recreating ritual from a feminist perspective can appear as a withdrawal from the real political struggle, given the historical association of ritual with the status quo. In the Netherlands, Women-Church has developed far more from political struggle than from groups meeting to develop liturgical celebrations. But the success of Elisabeth Fiorenza's model, 'the discipleship of equals', has been partly because this could give form to the political struggle; but mostly because in the Netherlands the Women and Faith Movement (Vrouw en Geloof Beweging) was already so strong.[8] This movement, on a national level, has been active particularly around issues such as incest, sexual violence and the distinctive rights of many marginalized groups, especially the plight of women forced into inescapable spirals of poverty. The success of Women-Church in finding authentic expression in The Netherlands is linked to the coincidental timing of the American inspiration with the need for the Vrouw en Geloof Beweging to acquire further conceptualizing.

A third expression of Women-Church – again American – can be seen as a compromise between the two models. Mary Hunt, a feminist ethicist, who with Dianne Neu runs WATER (Women's Association for Theology, Ethics and Ritual), sees Women-Church as groups of justice-seeking friends who together break word and sacrament.[9] When they launched 'Woman-Church in the Netherlands' in 1987, at the International Grail Centre, De Tiltenberg, in a creative and inspiring weekend, it was clear that for them ritual played a prominent part. This is a model of community more akin to the base-community model. Thus women – and women-identified men – meet together in basic community groups whose focus is commitment to justice for women and other marginalized groups. The challenge for Women-Church, it seems to me, is to encourage the fluidity and diversity of expression and development, remaining faithful to context, and faithful to the vision of 'from margin to centre', *always resisting the temptation to construct new centres of power and dominance.*

The second example of the search for redeeming community comes from the southern hemisphere. *Struggle to be the Sun Again* is the evocative title of Chung Hyun Kyung's book.[10] This is a clarion call to Asian women to rediscover and celebrate their own spirituality, and to cease being 'moons', which in this case symbolize dim reflections of what others – Europeans, the Church, men – have wanted them to be. No one who was present at the World Council of Churches' Assembly in Canberra, January 1991, who saw Professor Chung dance into the Assembly and heard her sermon 'Come, Holy Spirit!' could have doubted that a different image of Church was being offered. Life-centredness, inclusivity and action for justice are seen by Asian women theologians as the heart of Church.[11]

Mercy Amba Oduyoye, a Ghanaian theologian and Secretary to the World Council of Churches in Geneva, shows how this vision is part of the agenda of the Decade of the Churches in Solidarity with Women:

We as a Church will rise up and identify the obstacles to women's full and active participation in Church and society. We will work to remove the obstacles. We will affirm women's perspectives and contributions. We will pluck up and breakdown, build and plant. We will participate with God in transforming the world.[12]

Mercy Amba Oduyoye looks at the many initiatives taken in Africa, the Caribbean, Asia, Latin America, the Pacific and Europe. Her hopes that the commitment to ending the specific oppressions of poverty, the illiteracy of women, their violated sexuality and human dignity is the real concern of Church – what makes Church alive – give the concrete actualization of the cry 'Come Holy Spirit, renew the face of the earth!' This is the very authenticity of the resurrection message, as expressed by the Guatemalan poet, Julia Esquivel:

I would sacrifice myself, no matter how many times. I am no longer afraid of death – I die a thousand times and I am reborn another thousand times through that love from my people which nourishes hope.[13]

For my third example I come nearer home. Here in England Women in Theology (WIT) and the Catholic Women's Network (CWN) express both a commitment to the development of ritual and the struggle for justice.[14] The St Hilda Community is a Christian community, gathering weekly for worship, where inclusivity and mutuality in worship is given a powerful expression.[15] Many English Christian women belong, or identify themselves loosely with, all these groups, as well as with the Association of Inclusive Language, the St Joan's Alliance and with the development education of organizations like Christian Aid and Cafod.[16] But it is in the Movement for the Ordination of Women (MOW) that the anguish and the courage of women has been most clearly expressed.[17] It is important to draw out, now that the long travail has reached a successful conclusion, what the struggle has been saying to us about ecclesiology. Contrary to all that is being said about the supposed threat to Christian unity – which is insulting to those Churches in which women have ministered for a considerable time – the struggle within the Church of England to ordain women is loyal to authentic Church, the Church of 'the discipleship of equals', which Fiorenza claims is the original inspiration of the Jesus movement. Furthermore, the struggle is asserting a belief that the insights, gifts and ministry of women matter for the whole Church. *For Women-Church cannot remain marginal: to do so is to fail to transform culture, to hide one's light under a bushel, to fail to 'roll the stone away'* (the title of Mercy Oduyoye's book). Women are not trying to be 'the innocents of history' – forever identified with nature and not with culture – but to bring their experiences of a different manner of relating, a different experience of how power can be shared, a different articulation of life's deep experiences, to the moulding of renewed Christian community.

Those who criticize women for rocking the boat, for not keeping the peace, for disturbing order, fail to grasp the sheer power of women's love and loyalty for Church and faith in the transforming leaven of community. What is unseen is the pure generosity of service, the capacity to suffer for the realization of an ideal. For there is more than one category of martyrdom: too long have we understood the Christian martyr only as the one who is thrown to the lions or beheaded for the faith. There is a slow, unsung martyrdom of being ridiculed, trivialized, even demonized for struggling to incarnate a vision of community which threatens the mighty. Martyrdom can also be a compassionate, abiding identification with the throbbing heart of Christian community – God's longing for the wholeness of the earth. This witnessing-unto-death is fuelled by connection theology's understanding of God's Spirit.

RENEW THE FACE OF THE EARTH

The Spirit of this compassionate God has always been with us from the time of creation. God gave birth to us and the whole universe with her life-giving breath (*ruah*), the wind of life. This wind of life, this life-giving power of God is the Spirit which enabled people to come out of Egypt, resurrected Christ from death and started the Church as a liberative community. We also experience the life-giving Spirit of God in our people's struggle for liberation, their cry for life and the beauty and gift of nature. The Spirit of God has been teaching us through the 'survival wisdom' of the poor, the screams of the Han-ridden spirits of our people, and the blessings and curses of nature. Only when we can

hear this cry for life and can see the signs of liberation are we able to recognize the Holy Spirit's activity in the midst of suffering creation.
(Chung Hyun Kyung, Canberra 1991)

A renewed theology of the Spirit is the linking factor among the blossoming Christian feminist liberation communities. The Spirit of God, less linked to exclusively masculine imagery, experienced as breath of life, as the vitality of the rhythms of creation, as the force which leads to justice-making and as the memory connecting us with the suffering of our ancestors (*memoria passionis*), is the basis for Chung Hyun Kyung's passionate plea. In basing an ecclesiology on a renewed theology of the Spirit we are in fact reawakening an old intuition – *the Spirit is the Church*.[18] What this intuition expresses is not the identification of God's Spirit with the institution, but Spirit as the relational principle, searching for new manifestations of the gathered people of God.

There is, unfortunately, a reductive tendency today which tries to reduce the 'spirit-language' of the Gospels to language either about God the Father, or about Jesus.[19] To do so is to emphasize yet more strongly – and wrongly – that language and imagery of God are necessarily masculine. But to do the opposite, namely, to identify the Spirit as 'the feminine dimension of God' (Leonardo Boff), as our Mother (Yves Congar) brings us no further.[20] In fact, to see (as Boff does) an ontological link between women-Mary-Holy Spirit on the one hand, and men-Jesus on the other, is a dangerous dichotomy which threatens to undermine women's potential for imaging the Godhead in human form.[21] For the very Godhead is revealed as Mother, Jesus is our Mother (Julian of Norwich)! There is also a tendency to use mother-language itself in a reductive manner, again restricting the potential of women for imaging the divine. Often the spiritual qualities of motherhood are based on a patriarchal view of sexuality – the mother as 'empty vessel' receptive to the seed/word, never as actively co-creating in the conception process. It is always the tender, nurturing, caring and child-bearing aspects of motherhood which are emphasized. These are precisely the vulnerable aspects of being mother which frequently bring suffering to the lives of real mothers (see chapter 3). What is omitted from this imaging are mothers as strong and autonomous, mothers as figures of wisdom, mothers as culture-bearers. However, the image of the divine as mother is not the only way of imaging the divine as female . . . Nor can it ever fully encapsulate the power of the divine spirit.

If the theology of revelation being explored here has any force, then from the experience of liberating Christian community itself will emerge new understandings of the Holy Spirit. (That is, revelation arriving, not neatly-packaged from the past or from the skies, but from the blood, sweat and tears and delight of encountering God involved in all creation's travail.) The Spirit who blows where she will[22] can be trusted with new epiphany. And from the three examples of new community I have just described – by no means exhaustive – I believe such an epiphany is emerging.

Solidarity, mutuality, interdependence and commitment to the ongoing process of liberation are the very foundations of feminist Christian community. What is emerging from the experience of these groups is that it is in this very commitment to the liberation process that we experience a dynamism, a creative energy, an energy which connects. A theology of Spirit emerges as 'the energy of connectedness'.[23] The Spirit can be seen as the revelation of connection. Christian theology has often seen the Spirit as the bridging force who keeps us in contact with the message and presence of Jesus, as well as revealing its new dimensions.[24] That there is something relational, the binding force of community in the power of the Spirit has also been expressed.[25]

The Spirit works in a feminist theology of connection first of all as the energy which cracks open the discourse and the symbols by which we live, reaching out for what is suppressed, unheard, unarticulated. *The Spirit is the cry too deep for words* (Romans 8.26). Cracking open the restrictive discourse of separation and disengaged individualism creates space for the slow emergence of a new speech. Through the Spirit a hermeneutic of suspicion is cast on what has been defined and authorized as eternal truth, for the control of power over truth has to be made public again and again. If the emperor is wearing no clothes, we have to say so.

Christian theology has tamed and domesticated the Spirit,

129

restricting 'it' to the sacrament of Confirmation which itself, until recently, had lost touch with a richer theology of baptism. Its focus has been narrowly Christocentric and its prophetic and mystical dimensions have disappeared. But the Spirit as the revelation of connection sets free the Scriptures from imprisoning interpretations. For example, we are free to see Jesus in the full implications of Jewish messianic community; we are free to see 'saving power' – even saving relational power – as flowing from Judaism, rather than in opposition to it.[26]

The feminist chosen method of hearing into speech has cracked open a channel for the energies of connection to work. For hearing into speech is the work of authentic ecclesia: it is giving voice to the voiceless by creating safe places of trust and dialogue for the unheard stories to emerge. There is no way at the moment, given the impersonal character of most of the liturgies of established and mainstream Churches, that the stories of the victims of abuse, of homelessness, of racist discrimination are heard into speech, even though they may be given a nod in the prayers of intercession. The binding functions of true ecclesia are characterized by verbs of connection – by hearing, listening, responding, communing, reaching out and touching, by the mutuality of committing, cherishing, remembering and healing. The specific function of Spirit as energy of *connection* is, first, to heal the mistrust between Church and world, the spiritual and the profane. The words of Genesis can now be experienced in a liberating way: 'And the Spirit of God was moving over the face of the waters' (Gen. 1.2).

The creative Spirit of God is present to the whole of creation, to the whole of bodily, organic, sexual and psychological life. The Spirit is both our life-breath (Ps. 51) and the renewing life-energy of the cosmos (Ps. 104.30), the energizer of life and growth. Think of the dove who flew back to Noah in the Ark with an olive-tree twig in her mouth (Gen. 8.11). You can trust creation, the earth is your home, is her message – and she flew off, not to return. Do not build your holy places to escape creation or to hallow it. It is already Holy Being. Trust the Spirit to reveal ecological wisdom and healing connections. Being Church is being with the rhythms of creation, sharing its travail, and acting for its well-being.[27]

Could the Garden of Eden symbol in our tradition be recovered, not as a flight to a nostalgic non-existent Golden Age, an unspoilt Paradise, but as a call to responsibility for the ecological Garden of the World? Could the Church understand a call to mission as that of 'tending the Garden'? Could the call to metanoia or repentance be seen as an eleventh-hour chance to care for the wounded earth which we – the rich nations of the northern hemisphere – have plundered?

The Spirit as the energy of connection is also the raw elemental energy of communion, better expressed by the Hebrew *ruah* than by the Latin *spiritus* (with its implications of being untainted by matter).[28] Through the gathering of authentic community, the dynamics of encounter, the *ruah* of connection is made manifest. (Because of the shallow level of encounter of most Church liturgies, the *ruah* of connection does not get much chance to be effective.) I see the encounter with angels in the Scriptures as illuminating images from tradition of the Spirit driving to speech. In fact, Abraham's encounter with the angels outside his tent (Gen. 18) has become a much-loved example of the Triune God, imaged as love-in-mutual-relation (see the icon of the Russian painter, Andrei Rublev).

This becomes crystal clear in a Christian feminist interpretation of the annunciation (Luke 1.26–56). All crude, patriarchal interpretations should be resisted, such as Mary, the empty vessel, being impregnated by the Spirit, or Mary as having significance *only* as 'the mother of redemption'. Rather, we can see in the Gabriel–Mary story the energy of deepening connection, of mutuality and communion, where Mary's silence and listening was heard into speech. This was the speech of passionate response. It was immediately followed by an experience of community, in the visit to Elizabeth. Here the encounter acquired both communal and political meaning, in Elizabeth's recognition of the significance of the child and Mary's prophetic vision as to how God was acting on behalf of the oppressed peoples of Israel. It is not a revelation of the supernatural breaking into, intervening in, the (merely) human; it is the energy of connection which reveals God's purpose, in its personal, communal and political dimensions.

Similarly the role of the Spirit is to 'anoint into speech' the *prophets?*

stumbling, fearful, pain-filled word of the base communities in many parts of the world today. Here the anointing symbolism, a revered part of the traditional theology of the Spirit, takes on a new significance. In Johannine theology anointing is indwelling or abiding in the Spirit:

> but the anointing which you received from him abides in you, and you have no need that anyone should teach you; as his anointing teaches you about everything, and is true, and is no lie . . .
> (1 John 2.27)

Prophetic anointing in the Hebrew Scriptures is a commissioning to bring the good news to the broken-hearted (Isa. 61.1–2). Elisabeth Schüssler Fiorenza's book *In Memory of Her* took as inspiration the anointing story of Mark 14,[29] where an unnamed woman anointed Jesus, and he responded:

> 'Let her alone; why do you trouble her? She has done a beautiful thing to me. For you always have the poor with you, and whenever you will, you can do good to them; but you will not always have me. She has done what she could; she has anointed my body beforehand for burying. And truly, I say to you, wherever the gospel is preached in the whole world, what she has done will be told in memory of her'.
> (Mark 14.6–9)

The anointing performed by the woman here is a prophetic gesture enacted with the authority of someone who 'saw' the significance of Jesus. 'Anointing' expresses not only the commission to hear into speech the stories of suffering; it suggests that the role of the Spirit is to touch us at the core of our being, on the level of the archaic and instinctual – the level of the *jouissance* referred to by Julia Kristeva (see chapter 3). The Spirit can anoint into life the playful, joyful and ecstatic aspects of our personalities, the dimensions feared and suppressed by hierarchical ordering. Not that an orgiastic celebration of the irrational is being suggested: the Spirit of God is Holy Being. Abiding in the Spirit is to know in a connected manner. We can trust the Spirit to guide us through the ambiguity, through the savage forces which threaten the structural de-creation patterns discussed in the last chapter.

Anointing-in-the-Spirit is not just a metaphor for giving shape to what is formless, for not fleeing from the chaotic, messy and unruly aspects of personality and living, and for seeking for some means of integration: there is also a very concrete sacramentality of anointing, which is, in the manner of Women-Church ritual, to anoint with healing oils the flesh which has been abused; to anoint into life the damaged self-esteem, the person who has literally not been called into life or given value as a person. In other words the healing powers of anointing, through the Spirit as energy of connection, give prophetic, efficacious expression to 'I am the resurrection and the life'. This is the possibility that was denied to Dostoevsky's Sonia (see chapter 3).

Thus there are two dimensions being recovered by Christian feminist liberation community which may yet save Christian Church from irrelevance: namely, the prophetic and mystical dimensions. The absence of both of these stifles the power of religious community to act as leaven in society. Is it not true that the Spirit, as energy of connection, is revealing a new dimension of prophecy? From the situation of being a wilderness community, without power and status, the towers of patriarchy are being challenged by the clowns and fools of God, through the wisdom of Sophia. For the Church is called to be prophet as to where God is at home: God's home, God's *oikos* and sphere of activity (*oikonomia*) is the whole of creation. God is at home with the homeless of cardboard city; she is the rage for justice which keeps hope alive. Epiphany is celebrated in the liturgies at Peace Camps. For prophetic community, inspired by the Spirit as energy of connection, breaks down barriers, enters into dialogue with wisdoms of other faiths and receives divine ongoing communication through its rootedness in the earth – its humility – and its continuity with tradition seen as empowering, nurturing memory.

But, it will be argued, these prophetic groups have marginal status and, as such, will never transform society. It is the nature of prophecy to be rejected. Cassandra will never be heard.

There are two reasons why I believe that the prophetic dimension coming from Christian feminism carries hope for society. The first is that women are not quitters. Most justice groups who celebrate liturgies together have as their aim a society built on inclusive terms. They specifically oppose exclusive and separatist structures, even if women-only groups may always be necessary where women are victims of male violence. 'Hearing to speech' is ministry which women must always give to each other.

Despite the pain of exclusion and the damage of discrimination, the loyalty and love of women for Christian community is astounding. The Women-Church movement has generated an enormous confidence that when we are engaged in mutually healing activities, in peace-making, in protest against discrimination, in listening to stories of exclusion, we do this in the name of Church. When we reach across the boundaries and dialogue with our Jewish and Islamic sisters, we are loyal to a deeper ecumenism which believes that connection is stronger than difference. When we fight against the pain of exclusion, we are fighting for more than the inclusion of women in the ordained ministry. We struggle for the groups excluded from the eucharistic table, from intercommunion, for the poorer nations driven from their own land and from the means of decent human living. But we do this, faithful to the original vision of the Jesus movement which offered a new way of being and a new way of being at home in the universe. Listening to prophetic voices from the margins may yet offer the Church a way back to its own original inspiration.

ANOTHER MYSTICISM?

The second reason for believing that Christian feminism carries hope for the Church is through its recovery of a mystical dimension. It is undeniable that there is great enthusiasm today for 'mystical experiences' (whatever they are!). Much of what is happening can be classed under the heading of curiosity or obsession with the paranormal, or dabbling in signs and wonders. There is also a reaction from the rigid identification of the true with the empirically verifiable, and a flight from the exaggerated control of rationalism. The Church's obsession with power and control has been linked by some with her consistent condemning, or relegation to the sidelines, of the mystics. Matthew Fox, in *The Coming of the Cosmic Christ*, links the death of mysticism with the 'systemic crucifixion' of Mother Earth, of creativity, wisdom, youth, native peoples and with the dying of Mother

Church itself. The recovery of mysticism is seen by him as a 'resurrection story for our times' and he calls for the recovery of characteristics such as the playful, imagination, radical amazement, compassion, silence, and the birthing of images. He also cites 'feminist' as a category of mysticism, without it being at all clear what is meant by the term.[30]

It is undeniable that there is great enthusiasm today for the recovery of the mystics, including the medieval women mystics, among whom Hildegarde of Bingen must rate as the most popular.[31] Yet insufficient attention is given to what is meant by mysticism, by feminist mysticism, and whether we are using words about 'self' and 'spiritual experience' in the same way as the medieval mystics did. If not, what kind of difference does it make to how we understand mysticism? My major concern is to identify why a Christian feminist mysticism within connection theology is a hope-filled sign for the Church.

In *Redeeming the Dream* I followed the five-fold *via mystica* in terms of the feminist quest for self-discovery.[32] Here the focus is the community as locus for the new epiphany of the divine. The feminist mystic is in continuity with mystics of the Christian tradition in giving a central place to experience of the divine and in allowing her life to be shaped by this. However, the significance of the experience is never restricted to the individual but related to the community. One of the original insights of the feminist movement was that 'the personal is political'. World-view and concepts of self have changed almost beyond recognition from medieval times, and there is no way back to 'an original vision' (which was itself mediated by culture-determined images). Even the way 'experience' is understood has altered. We no longer believe in 'pure experience', the direct experience of God, but know that all experience is culturally mediated and interpreted by the symbols and images which shape our lives. This very shaking off of the power of the old images, concepts and symbols has created the empty spaces for the birthing of new images. Within the framework of the connected self which I have been developing the person is political, is spiritual, is mystical, and is political again. All things begin in mysticism, to end in politics, only to begin again, as the old saying goes.

Hence it is not surprising that the emergence of epiphanies of the divine are occurring in the political context of the struggle for justice. Calling on God, naming God from the depths, from our solidarity with the victims of oppression, as the power to re-connect, opens up the fathomless wellsprings of transcendence. God is immanent, God is transcendent, where this is seen as the power of crossing-over, the power to make deeper connections in justice. The transcendent God is experienced in the power, beauty and healing energy of the passion-for-justice-making.

In transcending the exclusive boundaries of language, of structures of ministry, in the creation of new symbols, rituals and ways of being, the floodgates of mystical imagery have been let loose. The sexual imagery – a familiar characteristic of the mystics, such as St John of the Cross – blossoms again, but in a renewed understanding of sexuality. The old penetrative model gives way to a model of mutual delight, of tenderness and vulnerability, of touching and being touched.[32]

This could never have happened without an exodus from patriarchal structures. Mysticism is at home in the Dark Night, in the empty spaces, in the chasms and fissures which the Spirit has cracked open for us. (Is it just an accident that the imagery of 'cracking open' suggests the egg, and thus the possibility of new life?) Yes, the feminist mystic experiences yearning for wholeness, but refuses to wallpaper the cracks, to fill them up with pseudo-meanings. Yes, it is important to stress again the playful, imaginative, the birthing of new images through dream, drama and song. But this will only have regenerative power for the Church as a whole if she will listen more deeply to the message of the mystic to let go, to let go of the obsessive need to control and dominate. Be not afraid of vulnerability, of powerlessness, of the body's mortality, of impotence in the face of the raging of the storm. Stay with the emptiness. Look at the faces of the suffering. And what will emerge? Like the child who puts a sea shell to her ear and hears the roar of the ocean, you will become attentive to the silent music. Sophia, God as wisdom, will reveal the hidden connections of your own Christian story.

10 A Revelation Story for our Times?

We last encountered Perceval in the amphitheatre in Delphi when he became aware of the tensions between Logos and Sophia – that is, the dominant myth of economic growth and success, which favours the powerful, in tension with an alternative view based on mutuality and just sharing for the most marginalized of peoples. The revelation on Mount Parnassus had the effect of throwing the Holy Fool back into his own story, to see it with new eyes, to pose questions he had never asked before. In this, the final chapter, we follow Perceval through the process of awakening consciousness. Through him we too confront our Christian story through the prism of a metaphor of connection.

ASKING NEW QUESTIONS

Perceval stood at the top of Glastonbury Tor, gazing down at the plains of the vale of Avalon which rolled away into the mists of the horizon. Here, for him, lay the heart of the mystery.[1] This piece of earth, sacred to Christendom – and to religions which preceded it – held treasured memories for him. He had never devoted much time to the founding inspiration of the shrine of Glastonbury – to the voyage of Joseph of Arimathea, bringing the Holy Cup of the Last Supper . . . Joseph, from whose staff, it is said, had blossomed the famous Glastonbury Thorn, and from whose faithful band of followers would spring the legend and company of the Grail. It was rather the court of King Arthur which had formed the horizon of Perceval's world, the dream of the Fellowship of the Round Table and the search for the Holy Grail. But the dream had gone sadly awry. Rivalries and obsession with military conquest had shattered the fellowship of the once-and-future King.

Looking down at Glastonbury Abbey below, Perceval now realized how far he had come from his original vision. He had sought wisdom, the wisdom which would bring about the healing of the land and justice among the peoples of the world. He had sought it first through asceticism, through renunciation of the natural world and his own sexuality; then from the fellowship at Arthur's court and from the spirituality of the monks at Glastonbury. Not only had he not found it, but he had participated in a system which had lost all touch with ecological wholeness. He had wasted years seeking the Holy Grail in heavenly spheres, and become blind to the cup of suffering on this earth which cried out for attention.

But Perceval had experienced a moment of revelation. His recent travelling through the world revealed a devastation beyond anything he had ever imagined. That there could be desertification of once fertile land and de-forestation on such a vast scale, sickened him. That there could be such full-scale indifference to the plight of the poor, indigenous peoples driven from their land and such single-minded pursuit of wealth and power revolted the very depths of his being. Time was running out for life on earth, he thought. Truly a time of 'apocalypse now'. He had failed, we have all failed, he realized, to ask the right question. And in a second moment of revelation, *he made the connections* . . . He saw, with all the crystal clarity of the water in the Chalice Well, that the logic and prevailing interpretation of his own Christian belief was part of the problem.

He looked down at the valley. The Glastonbury Lake village was no more, and the island of Avalon was but a memory. We drove Avalon into the mists . . . The Little People were driven from their land, he thought. With the might of the sword we suppressed any trace of the old, Goddess religion. We demonized her priestesses into witches. We were afraid of anything which suggested that the body was holy. We survived by excluding: we banished the Celtic peoples to the corners of what we, the conquerors, called the 'civilized' world; we banished the religion of the mother to Avalon and drastically cut down the influence of women within Christianity itself.[2] The power of the female was made invisible; we became blind even to intuiting it in our Scripture and tradition and eradicated it from our language.

And what has happened? We saw divine revelation as set squarely in the heavens; we set out questing on horseback for a

Cup whose vision was removed from us. We imagined that God removed it because we were too impure and unworthy for the heavenly vision. We busily created our élitist priesthood through the ages, preserving a mystique about 'the mysteries'. We built our towers and cathedrals, all aiming upwards for the heavens. We created liturgies solidifying our exclusivist vision.

All the time, the life-blood of the Holy Grail was being poured out on earth anew by the suffering of those we had excluded. For the fools of history have drunk from the Cup. Francis of Assisi, the *jongleur* of Notre Dame, those who celebrate in the *favelas* and barrios of Latin America, despite the overwhelming poverty and injustice, have witnessed to the truth of the Holy Grail which its own knights had missed. For the Grail Cup is a symbol of sharing, of the commitment to the discovery of the pattern which connects. The Fellowship of the Grail is the inclusive community of the prophetic witness to God's justice. And the real mystery is God's presence here on earth among us, in all the glory and mess of human and non-human experience!

Perceval began the descent towards the Abbey with a heavy heart. He could see far away the factory chimneys alongside the river Severn, flowing into the Bristol Channel. Bristol – formerly one of the ports for the African slave-trade. He thought of the pollution of rivers, the contaminated waters, the children dying of leukaemia as a result of radiation from nuclear power stations. The knights of the Holy Grail had failed. What hope was there that he could look again at the Christian story as offering healing to the brokenness of the contemporary world? How was God speaking to a world ravaged by the greed and dominance of the rich nations, a world planning to re-form after the death of communism according to the capitalist dream?

DRINKING FROM THE WELLS OF SALVATION

Darkness was falling as Perceval entered the Gardens of the Chalice Well. He had forgotten that the waters still flowed, and that people still came to drink from the ancient source of water, crystal-clear from the heart of the mountain – but with a hint of red, suggestive of blood. With joy you shall draw water from the wells of salvation, he thought, and knelt to drink. A woman from the village turned and offered him a cup of water. He accepted the cup gratefully and in the act of drinking found himself opening up to a new realization. Jesus accepts water from the Samaritan woman (John 4) and prophesies that the water which he will give will well up for eternal life (John 4.14). The Holy Fool, through the ministering act of simple kindness of a woman, recovers hope in the sacredness of creation.

Then the third moment of revelation occurred. Perceval knew with every fibre of his being that God's presence irradiates the world – this Garden, this flowing spring, these tired dirty feet, these stones, all the suffering and loving which is going on and which will go on in this town. And as the woman's wise, steady eyes never wavered, it was as if the text of the Book of Revelation was being proclaimed anew, for him, for the dream of beloved community, for today's situation, for apocalypse now:

> And a great portent appeared in heaven, a woman clothed with the sun, with the moon under her feet, and on her head a crown of twelve stars; she was with child, and she cried out in her pangs of birth, in anguish for delivery. And another portent appeared in heaven, behold, a great dragon . . . His tail swept down a third of the stars of heaven, and cast them to the earth. And the dragon stood before the woman who was about to bear a child, that he might devour her child when she brought it forth; she brought forth a male child, one who is to rule all nations with a rod of iron, but her child was caught up to God, and to his throne, and the woman fled into the wilderness, where she has a place prepared by God, in which to be nourished for one thousand two hundred and sixty days.
> (Rev. 12.1–6)

Perceval saw that he had always read and understood the story with the eyes of Logos. It had been for him predominantly a story of separation.[3] The woman and the dragon were absolute enemies. Her child, once born, is snatched away from her, to be with God and prepare to rule with a rod of iron; that rod of iron, symbolic of Roman imperial might, which now symbolized the threatened imposition of 'new world order'. So the child has no mother, and a mother grieves over a missing child . . .

Perceval realized that he had been at home in this story because it was a world which he recognized. He himself had abandoned a grieving mother for a world in which disaster threatened to overwhelm, and for which the only answer had been to conquer the enemy with military force.

But suppose the story offers an epiphany of connection for our times? Suppose it can be read with the logic of connected knowing, and with the eyes of Sophia?

EXODUS NOW: SOPHIA RETURNS FROM THE WILDERNESS

As long as we read the text of Revelation 12 with the eyes of Logos, the woman will remain in the wilderness, separate from her child, who is being groomed, as was Perceval, for military conflict. The child, writes Catherine Keller, has been co-opted by patriarchal rule. But who is she really, this woman? Is she Sophia, or Earth Mother, Mary, or a figure of the Church? What insights can a new reading bring?

In the first place, it is important to understand that to see her as Mary, or as figure of the Church (an interpretation still popular today), is actually a late medieval reading of the text. It is one reading among many and a confining one at that. All these readings are responses to particular questions. Whether we see her – in a Jewish interpretation – as the New Israel, in the pains of giving birth,[4] or as a Mother Goddess linked with Artemis, Isis or Leto,[5] or as the nucleus of the nation, salvaged from the ruins of Jerusalem, we look to her as a figure of divine revelation, the first among seven signs of the Book of Revelation, and as an answer to the questions, the anguish we feel about our own situation.

I see her (as Catherine Keller does), not as Eternal Woman, but as an epiphany of Sophia, the wisdom of God consistently imaged as female. She is the revelation of the victimization of the female under patriarchy. Her exile is our exile. Her marginalization (chapter 1) is that of the many groups excluded from society. She represents the Exodus of the woman – like Hagar – to the desert: vulnerable, pregnant, with creative vitalizing energies which society rejects. Like Psyche of the ancient legend, she wanders, suffering and pregnant.[6]

141

Like Psyche, too, she is befriended by nature – the ants and the talking reeds – when all human help fails. *She is an epiphany of the connectedness of creation*: the desert receives her and is experienced by her as a place of nourishment. When the serpent/dragon threatens to destroy her and the baby, she is carried away on an eagle's wings (symbolic of the Shekinah, or presence of God?). Still threatened by the serpent, the earth comes to her rescue, opens its mouth and swallows the river which the dragon had poured from its mouth (Rev. 12.16).

If she is an epiphany of connectedness, why then is she an enemy of the serpent/dragon? This is in marked contrast to Eve, where Eve is in conversation with the serpent (Gen 3.1–6). This, I believe, is a tragic indication of the consequences of broken connection: communication with the animal world is lost. Whatever is 'beastly' is demonized, scapegoated and rejected. This story, set as it is in a time of escalating catastrophe, is a powerful image of the effects of separation (see chapter 4). Between the two episodes about the Woman (Rev. 12.1–6, 13–17), we are given the dramatic cosmic battle, where the archangel Michael defeats the dragon and his angels, and they are cast out of heaven. There is no place for the dragon/serpent/satan in heaven. Heaven and earth, good and evil are depicted as in total opposition to each other. One victim of such a confrontation is the communication between human and animal. Is there even a hint that the serpent/dragon desires to re-establish contact – in his persistent haunting of the woman, and stated intention of making war on the rest of her offspring? Does the dragon represent the demonized part of human nature that forever seeks integration?

The woman is an image of the divine, and an epiphany of connection in a more profound sense. In this book I have been exploring an understanding of divine communication arising from a world-view based on connection. I have suggested that revelation is less the unveiling of a set of eternal truths delivered from on high, than the *Offenbarung*, the opening of the ears, to how God relates to us through all the organic connectedness of creation. It is an opening-up to all the creative possibilities of a future for our planet. The woman, Sophia, rooted in connectedness with all creation, expressing creative, birth-giving vitality, is the answer to the questions of

Perceval. She represents hope for the wounded earth and for 'apocalypse now', because she does not envision the fashioning of new heaven and new earth as other-worldly utopia, but as the ethical priority here-and-now. She hears the silent into speech and is the one who listens to unheard cries. She challenges any rigid, imperialistic 'new world order' based on exclusion of the 'other', and of the fluid, chaotic stream of enriching possibilities.

Sophia, the woman of Revelation 12, is also a figure of the divine in that, like Christ, she suffers and is innocent. She is a prophetic figure, suffering so that new creation is made flesh. She is mystical in the profundity of her connection and union with God. She does not have to 'struggle to be the sun again' (the title of Chung Hyun Kyung's book). She is clothed in the sun with the moon at her feet – in other words, with all the trappings of a goddess. But her heavenly glory does not separate her from the earth. She is the hope for marginalized community because, as epiphany of prophetic-mystic community, she is the revelation for today that the long exile and waiting is over, new voices are heard in the wilderness, and women may safely leave the desert and be the leaven for beloved community.

The Holy Fool has asked his question. As the Woman emerges from the wilderness of exile, of absence and exclusion from 'mainstream' theological tradition, into a world starved of hope, Perceval recedes into the mists of history.

Notes

Introduction

1 Harvey Cox, *The Feast of Fools: A Theological Essay on Festivity and Fantasy* (New York, Harper & Row, 1969), p. 3.
2 See Rosemary Haughton, *Tales from Eternity* (London, Allen and Unwin, 1973), 'The youngest Son', pp. 19–49.

Chapter 1: Seeking the Right Question

1 Important sources for the Grail legend and the story of Perceval (Parsifal) are: Sir Thomas Malory, *La Morte d'Arthur*, London, Headline, 1961; Wolfram von Eschenbach, *Parsifal*, London, Penguin, 1980, tr. A. T. Hatto; Chrétien de Troyes, *Arthurian Romances*, London, Dent, 1987. For a more recent collection of articles see John Matthews, ed., *The Household of the Grail*, Wellingborough, The Aquarian Press, 1990.
2 George Eliot, *Middlemarch*, Boston, Houghton Mifflin, 1956.
3 Post-modernism is a philosophical 'current' – not a movement – which challenges the great overarching universalist interpretations of history, culture and identity. It emphasizes instead partial meaning, and the influence of context, positional thinking and perspective on philosophical analysis. See Jonathan Culler, *On Deconstruction: Theory and Criticism after Structuralism*, London, Routledge & Kegan Paul, 1983; Jean-François Lyotard, *The Post-modern Condition: A Report on Knowledge*, Manchester, Manchester University Press, 1984. The feminist position vis à vis post-modernism is complex: see Sabina Lovibond, 'Feminism and Postmodernism', in *New Left Review* 1989, pp. 5–28.
4 See Mary Grey, 'Europe is a Sexist Myth', *Concilium*, April 1992, pp. 12–19.
5 See John Robinson, *Honest to God* (London, SCM Press, 1964) for discussion of 'the beyond in our midst' in Tillich and Bonhoeffer.
6 'It is possible to outline the general shape of women's living conditions in the rural areas of the third world. They share, first of all, their poverty; roughly 75% of the world's population are among the poorest, and women make up the majority of the poor . . . Time-budgets show that women not only perform physically heavier work, but also work longer hours than men.' Irene Dankelman and Joan Davidson, *Women and the Environment in the Third World* (London, Earthscan, 1988), p. 3; 'Although women represent half the world's population and one-third of the official labour force, they receive only one per cent of the world

145

Notes

income and own less than one per cent of the world's property.' (UN conference, Copenhagen, 1980), quoted in Dankelman and Davidson, p. 5.

7 Justice, Peace and Integrity of Creation (JPIC) refers to the Conciliar Process of the World Council of Churches, inaugurated in Basel, Switzerland in May 1989. For background, history and theology see Joseph Selling, 'The "Conciliar Process" for Justice, Peace and the Integrity of Creation: The European Experience', *Louvain Studies* April 1989, pp. 346–64.

8 These are the closing lines of the carol *It came upon the midnight clear*, by E. H. Sears (1810–1876).

9 Adrienne Rich, 'Transcendental Etude', in *The Dream of a Common Language* (New York, Norton, 1978), p. 73.

10 See Martin Buber, *I and Thou*, Edinburgh, T & T Clark, 1970, tr. W. Kaufmann.

Chapter 2: Woman: Silent Outsider to Revelation

1 For Hagar see Phyllis Trible, 'The Desolation of Rejection', in *Texts of Terror* (Philadelphia, Fortress, 1984), pp. 9–35; Elsa Tamez, 'The Woman who Complicated the History of Salvation' in John Pobee and Barbel von Wartenberg-Potter, eds., *New Eyes for Reading* (Geneva, World Council of Churches, 1986), pp. 3–17.

2 Judith Plaskow, *Standing Again at Sinai: Judaism from a Feminist Perspective*, San Francisco, Harper & Row, 1990.

3 In the Roman Catholic Church this inspiration springs from the recovery of the image in the Vatican Council Dogmatic Constitution on the Church, *Lumen Gentium* (November 1964). See Austin Flannery, ed., *The Documents of Vatican II*, New York, Costello; Dublin, Dominican Publications, 1975; Willem Bekkers, *God's People on the Way*, London, Burns & Oates, 1966, tr. Catherine Jarrott.

4 Rosemary Ruether, *Women-Church: Theology and Practice* (New York, Harper & Row, 1985), p. 72. (See discussion in Ch. 8.)

5 Avery Dulles, *Models of Revelation*, New York, Doubleday, 1983. (See especially chs. 3–7.)

6 For the problem of doctrinal development see Nicholas Lash, *Change in Focus: A Study of Doctrinal Change and Continuity*, London, Sheed & Ward, 1973.

7 Dulles, pp. 53–67.

8 James Cone, *My Soul Looks Back* (New York, Orbis, 1986), pp. 121–2.

9 On the problem of women's invisibility in the periodicization of history see Elisabeth Schüssler Fiorenza, 'Justified by All her Children: Struggle, Memory and Vision', in *Concilium*, February 1990, p. 21.

10 See the clear description of the origins of romantic feminism – also known as 'cultural feminism' – in Maria Riley, *Transforming Feminism* (Washington D.C., Sheed & Ward, 1989), pp. 50–2.

11 George Eliot, *Middlemarch*, (Boston, Houghton Mifflin, 1956), p. 287.

See my discussion in *Redeeming the Dream* (London, SPCK; Mystic, CT, Twenty-Third Publications, 1989), pp. 58–60.

12 For a useful modern study of Hildegarde see B. Newman, *Sister of Wisdom: St Hildegard's Theology of the Feminine*, Berkeley, Scholars Press, 1987; also Fiona Bowie and Oliver Davies, eds., *Hildegarde of Bingen: An Anthology*, London, SPCK; New York, Crossroad, 1990.

13 See Caroline Walker Bynum, '". . . And Woman His Humanity": Female Imagery in the Religious Writing of the Later Middle Ages', in *Gender and Religion: On the Complexity of Symbols* (Boston, Beacon Press, 1986), pp. 257–88.

14 For the challenge of verifiability see A. Flew and A. MacIntyre, eds., *New Essays in Philosophical Theology*, London, SCM Press, 1955. For a defence of religious language in the face of the verifiability problem see E. Mascall, *Words and Images*, London, Longman, Green and Co., 1957.

15 There is proliferating literature on the Goddess, as well as on the links between Mary and the pre-Christian Goddess religions. See Ian Begg, *The Cult of the Black Virgin*, London, Routledge & Kegan Paul, 1985; Elinor W. Gadon, *The Once-and-Future Goddess*, Wellingborough, The Aquarian Press, 1990.

16 Mary Field Belenky, Blythe McVicker Clinchy, Nancy Rule Goldberger and Jill Mattuck Tarule, eds., *Women's Ways of Knowing: The Development of Self, Voice and Mind*, New York, Basic Books, 1986.

17 See Trible, *Texts of Terror*, pp. 65–91.

18 Belenky et al., *Ways of Knowing*, pp. 32–51.

19 ibid., pp. 52–86.

20 ibid., p. 61.

21 Paul Tillich, 'You are Accepted', in *The Shaking of the Foundations* (London, Penguin, 1962), p. 161: 'Thus, the state of our whole life is estrangement from others and ourselves, because we are estranged from the Ground of our Being, because we are estranged from the origin and aim of our life. We are separated from the mystery, the depth and the greatness of our existence . . .'

22 William Wordsworth, 'The World is too much with us', in *Poems* ed. Matthew Arnold (London, Macmillan (1879) 1960), p. 214.

23 David Tracy, 'On Naming the Present', *Concilium*, 1990/1, pp. 66–85.

24 The quotation is from 'Natural Resources', in *The Dream of a Common Language* (New York, Norton, 1978) p. 66; the wish to be washed free of the guilt of words is from 'The Images' in *A Wild Patience has taken me Thus Far* (New York, Norton, 1981), p. 4.

25 The phrase, which has now become commonplace, was first used by the then Cabinet Secretary Sir Robert Armstrong during the *Spycatcher* affair.

26 Belenky et al., *Ways of Knowing*, pp. 100–30.

Chapter 3: Living the Sacrifice and the Lost Experience of Women

1 Fyodor Dostoevsky, *Crime and Punishment* (London, J. M. Dent, 1911), p. 267. Subsequent quotes on pages 261, 266, 454 and 456 of this edition.

2 On this point see Deirdre David, *Intellectual Women and Victorian Patriarchy*, London, Macmillan, 1987. (The discussion centres on George Eliot, Harriet Martineau and Elizabeth Barrett Browning.)

3 See M. Grey, ' "Yet Women Will be saved through bearing Children" (1 Tim. 2.15): Motherhood and the Possibility of a Contemporary Discourse for Women', *Bijdragen, Tijdschrift voor Filosofie en Theologie* 52 (1991), pp. 58–69.

4 Luise Schotroff, 'Letter to Adam', in *Lieve Adam, Beste David* (Baarn, Ten Have, 1989), p. 9 (my translation).

5 See Mary E. Hunt, *Fierce Tenderness: A Feminist Theology of Friendship*, New York, Crossroad, 1991.

6 Mercy Amba Oduyoye, 'Poverty and Motherhood', *Concilium*, December 1989, p. 26.

7 See Dorry de Beijer, 'Motherhood and the New Forms of Reproductive Technology: Passive Source of Nutrition and Rational Consumer', *Concilium*, ibid., pp. 73–81. Also, Adrienne Rich, *Of Woman Born*, New York, Bantam, 1976.

8 Elizabeth Fox-Genovese, *Feminism Without Illusions: A Critique of Individualism* (Chapel Hill and London, University of North Carolina Press), p. 138.

9 In other words, changing *teknogonia* (the bearing of children) to *teknotrophia* (the rearing of children).

10 John Calvin, *Commentary on II Corinthians, Timothy, Titus and Philemon*, tr. T. A. Smail, Edinburgh, Oliver & Boyd, 1964.

11 Jerome, *Against Jovinian*, 1.47, Nicene and Post-Nicene Fathers 6. See the discussion of this point in Margaret Miles, *Carnal Knowing: Female Nakedness and Religious Meaning in the Christian West* (New York, Vintage Books, 1989), ch. 2.

12 Mary Daly, *Gyn/Ecology* (Boston, Beacon Press, 1978), quoting Rich, *Of Woman Born*, p. 168.

13 Albert Barnes, *Notes*, London, Blackie and Sons, 1832.

14 William Barclay, *The Pastoral Epistles*, Edinburgh, St Andrew's Press, (1956) 1975.

15 See *The Cambridge New Testament: The Pastoral Epistles* (Cambridge, Clay, 1899), pp. 49–50.

16 *Mulieris Dignitatem: Apostolic Letter of Pope John Paul II on the Dignity and Vocation of Women* (London, Catholic Truth Society, 1988), p. 15.

17 ibid., p. 17.

18 ibid., p. 68.

19 ibid., p. 71.

20 Julia Kristeva, 'About Chinese Women', in Toril Moi, ed., *The Kristeva Reader* (Oxford, Blackwell, 1986), pp. 138–59.

21 Kristeva, 'Revolution in Poetic Language', in *The Kristeva Reader*, p. 95.

22 Kristeva, 'About Chinese Women', pp. 141–2. 'The unity which is represented by the God of monotheism is sustained by a desire that pervades the community, a desire which is at once stirring and threatening. Remove this threatening desire . . . from man, place beside him and create a supplement for what is lacking in this man who speaks to

his God; and you have woman, who has no access to the word, but appears as pure desire to seize it . . .'. See also p. 153.

23 Seteney Shami, 'Feminine Identity and Ethnic Identity: the Case of the Circassians in Jordan', paper given at the Congress, in *Who's Afraid of Femininity?* University of Nijmegen, The Netherlands, 1991; publication forthcoming.

24 Kristeva, 'About Chinese Women', p. 141.

25 ibid.

26 See Saskia de Jong, *Onvruchtbare Moeders: Een Feministische Lezing van Genesis*, Boxtel, Katholieke Bijbel Stichting, 1989; Fokkelien Van Dijk-Hemmes, 'En Sara Lachte: Exegetische Overwegingen rond het bijbelverhaal over Sara', *Wending* 1981, pp. 684–91.

27 See Kristeva, 'Semiotics of Biblical Abomination', in *Powers of Horror* (New York, Columbia University Press), p. 100.

28 Phyllis Trible, 'The Daughter of Jephthah: An Inhuman Sacrifice', in *Texts of Terror*, p. 104.

29 Kristeva, 'Stabat Mater', in *The Kristeva Reader*, p. 165.

30 Mary Daly, 'The Qualitative Leap', *Quest*, April 1975, p. 126.

31 Kristeva, 'About Chinese Women', p. 158.

32 Kristeva, 'Women's Time', in *The Kristeva Reader*, p. 200.

33 Kristeva, 'About Chinese Women', p. 156.

34 See, for example, Ivone Gebara and Maria Clara Bingemer, *Mary, Mother of God, Mother of the Poor*, New York, Orbis, 1989; Mary Grey, 'Reclaiming Mary: A Task for Feminist Theology', *The Way* April 1989, pp. 335–40; Els Maeckelberghe, *Desperately Seeking Mary*, Kampen, The Netherlands, Kok, 1991; Rosemary Ruether, *Mary: The Feminine Face of the Church*, London, SCM Press, 1979.

35 George Eliot, *Romola*, (1863) London, Penguin, 1980.

36 ibid., p. 578.

37 ibid., p. 590.

38 ibid., p. 590.

INTERMEZZO: Cassandra, Voice from the margins

1 Christa Wolf, *Cassandra*, London, Virago, 1984, p. 36.

2 See *The Fourth Dimension: Interviews with Christa Wolf* intro. Karin McPherson (London and New York, Verso, 1988), ch. 10.

3 Wolf, *Cassandra*, p. 36.

4 ibid., p. 38.

5 ibid., pp. 38–9.

6 ibid., p. 97.

7 'This above all, to choose not to be victim' is the conclusion of the protagonist of Margaret Atwood's novel *Surfacing* (London, Virago, 1979), p. 191; see my *Redeeming the Dream*, p. 15.

8 For this word and for some helpful reflections on Cassandra I am grateful to Petra Von Morstein, 'A Message from Cassandra – Experience and Knowledge: Dichotomy and Unity', in Lorraine Code, Sheila Mullett and Christine Overall, eds., *Feminist Perspectives: Philosophical Essays on*

Method and Morals (Toronto, University of Toronto Press, 1988), pp. 46–83.
9 Wolf, *Cassandra*, p. 127.
10 ibid., p. 51.
11 ibid., p. 59.
12 ibid., p. 57.
13 ibid., p. 57.
14 Wolf, *Cassandra*, p. 107.
15 ibid., p. 133.
16 ibid., p. 60.
17 Chung Hyun Kyung, '"Han-pu-ri": Doing Theology from Korean Women's Perspective', in Virginia Fabella and Sun Ai Lee Park, eds., *We Dare to Dream* (Kow Loon, Hong Kong, Asian Women's Resource Centre, 1989), pp. 141–2.
18 Wolf, *Cassandra*, p. 21.

Chapter 4: Connectedness as New Metaphor for Christian Revelation

1 Adrienne Rich, 'The Spirit of Place', in *A Wild Patience has Taken me Thus Far* (New York, Norton, 1981), p. 45.
2 I have discussed this, and other points relating to this chapter, in M. Grey, 'Claiming Power-in-Relation: Exploring the Ethics of Connection' *Journal of Feminist Studies in Religion* January 1991, pp. 7–18; 'Ethics of Connection or Politics of Difference'?, paper given at the Congress, *Who's Afraid of Femininity?* University of Nijmegen, Netherlands, 1991; publication forthcoming.
3 Carter Heyward, *The Redemption of God: a Theology of Mutual Relation*, Washington D.C., University of America Press, 1982.
4 M. Grey, *Redeeming the Dream*, London, SPCK; Mystic, CT, Twenty-Third Publications, 1989.
5 Catherine Keller, *From a Broken Web*, Boston, Beacon Press, 1986.
6 Howard Clinebell, *Healing Ourselves/Healing the Planet – An Object Relations/Creation Theology Approach to Ecological Pastoral Care and Counselling*, paper given at Congress of Pastoral Care and Counselling, Noordwijkerhout, The Netherlands, 1991.
7 Rita Nakashima Brock, *Journeys by Heart: A Christology of Erotic Power*, New York, Crossroad, 1988.
8 Keller, pp. 216–52; Jean Sinday, 'The Spider's Web of Triple Oppression', in Musimbi Kanyoro and W. Robins, eds., *The Power We Celebrate* (Geneva, Lutheran World Federation, 1992), p. 29.
9 Adrienne Rich, 'Integrity', in *A Wild Patience*, p. 9.
10 Alice Walker, *The Color Purple* (New York, Harcourt, Brace, Jovanovich, 1982; London, Women's Press, 1983), p. 167.
11 Charles Taylor, *Sources of the Self* (Cambridge, Cambridge University Press, 1989) defines the relevance of the idea of 'epiphany' for creative works of art in two ways. The first is when a work of art portrays something – unspoilt nature or an emotion, for example – in such a way as

to show some greater significance shining through. (Think of Wordsworth and the Romantics.) The second way – belonging more to the twentieth century – shifts the locus of epiphany to the work itself (Taylor, p. 419). In a book which tries to show that human experience of connectedness is a locus for revelation, I rely more on Taylor's second type, but widen the idea of text or work of art to embodiments of 'the pattern which connects'.

12 Catharina Halkes, *New Creation: Christian Feminism and the Renewal of the Earth*, London, SPCK; Louisville, KY, Westminster/John Knox Press, 1991.

13 Anne Primavesi, *From Apocalypse to Genesis: Ecology, Feminism and Christianity*, London, Burns & Oates, 1991.

14 The work of Thomas Berry is notable in this respect: see Anne Lonergan and Caroline Richards, eds., *Thomas Berry and the New Cosmology* (Mystic, CT, Twenty-Third Publications, 1992); Anne Lonergan and Stephen Dunn, eds., *Befriending the Earth*, Mystic, CT, Twenty-Third Publications, 1992. See also Janet Martin Soskice, 'Creation and Revelation', *Theology* January 1991, pp. 31–8.

15 See *Redeeming the Dream*, ch. 3.

16 Elisabeth Schüssler Fiorenza, *In Memory of Her*, London, SCM Press, 1983, and *Bread not Stone: The Challenge of Biblical Scholarship*, Boston, Beacon Press, 1984.

17 Alice Walker, *Meridian*, London, The Women's Press, 1982.

18 ibid., p. 38.

19 Toni Morrison, *Tar Baby* (London, Grafton Books, 1983), p. 273.

20 Walker, *Meridian*, p. 50.

21 ibid., pp. 50–1.

22 ibid.

23 Chung Hyun Kyung, *Struggle to be the Sun Again* (London, SCM Press, 1990), p. 39ff.

24 Chung Hyun Kyung, *Come, Holy Spirit*, Canberra, World Council of Churches, 1990.

25 Chung Hyun Kyung, *Struggle*, p. 40.

26 Marta Benavides, 'My Mother's Garden is a New Creation', in Letty Russell and Kwok Pui Lan, eds., *Inheriting our Mothers' Gardens* (Louisville, KY, Westminster, 1988), pp. 136ff.

Chapter 5: The Separate Self and the Denial of Relation

1 Adrienne Rich, 'Phantasia for Elvira Shatayev', in *The Dream of a Common Language* (New York, Norton, 1978), p. 6.

2 Catherine Keller, *From a Broken Web*, Boston, Beacon Press, 1986; see ch. 4.

3 Charles Taylor, *Sources of the Self*, Cambridge, Cambridge University Press, 1989.

4 For a good introduction to French feminism, see Toril Moi, ed., *French Feminist Thought*, Oxford, Blackwell, 1987.

Notes

5 George Steiner, *Real Presences* (London, Faber and Faber, 1991), pp. 206–7.

6 ibid., p. 207.

7 See especially Carol Gilligan, *In a Different Voice? Psychological Theory and Women's Development*, Cambridge, MA, Harvard University Press, 1982.

8 Carol Gilligan, 'Remapping the Moral Domain: New Images of Self in Relationship', in Carol Gilligan, Janie Victoria Ward and Jill McClean Taylor, eds., *Mapping the Moral Domain* (Cambridge, MA, Harvard University Press, 1988), pp. 3–19.

9 ibid., p. 4.

10 'Jerome paints a highly-coloured picture of her departure, (to Jerusalem) with her kinsfolk, her elder daughter and her little boy Toxotius sobbing on the quay, while "she herself turned her dry eye heavenwards, overcoming her love for her children by her love for God"': J. N. D. Kelly, *Jerome* (London, Duckworth, 1975), p. 117. For Latin text see Jerome, *Letter* 108 (in fact an epitaph on Paula's life), PL 22 (Paris, Migne, 1877), p. 878.

11 Elaine Scarry, *The Body in Pain: The Making and Unmaking of the World*, New York and Oxford, Oxford University Press, 1985.

12 For example, in M. Grey, 'Weaving New Connections: the Promise of Process Thought for Christian Theology, Inaugural Lecture, University of Nijmegen, Holland, February 1989.

13 See Paul Davies, *God and the New Physics*, London, Dent, 1983; Arthur Koestler, *Janus*, London, Hutchinson, 1978; Fritjof Capra, *The turning Point: Science, Society and the Rising Culture*, New York, Simon and Schuster, 1982.

14 For Edward Echlin, see *The Christian Green Heritage: The World as Creation*, Bramcote, Notts, Grove Books, 1989; 'Christian Wholeism within Creation under God, *The Month*, November 1990, pp. 450–7. 'Let's Re-enter God's Creation Now', *The Month*, August 1991, pp. 359–64. For Thomas Berry, see ch. 4, n. 14.

15 Keller, *Broken Web*, p. 192.

16 See Judith V. Jordan, Alexandra G. Kaplan, Jean Baker Miller, Irene P. Stiver and Janet L. Surrey, *Women's Growth in Connection: Writings from the Stone Center*, New York and London, The Guilford Press, 1991.

17 Ruth Page in *Ambiguity and the Presence of God* (London, SCM Press, 1985) explores the notion of ambiguity. See further, in connection with evil and the image of God, ch. 7 of this book.

18 Joanna Macy, 'Awakening to the Ecological Self', in Judith L. Plant, ed., *Healing the Wounds: The Promise of Eco-feminism*, (Philadelphia, New Society, 1989), p. 205.

19 ibid., p. 207.

20 ibid. Some of these ideas are developed in the context of a meditation workshop, in Joanna Macy, 'Despair and Empowerment Work', in Tilden H. Edwards, ed., *Living with Apocalypse* (San Francisco, Harper & Row, 1984), pp. 117–33.

21 Rich, 'Transcendental Etude', in *The Dream of a Common Language*, pp. 74–5.
22 ibid., pp. 76–7.
23 Annie Dillard, *Pilgrim at Tinker Creek*, New York, Harper & Row, 1985.
24 Jim Cheney, ' "The Waters of Separation": Myth and Ritual in Annie Dillard's "Pilgrim at Tinker Creek" ', *Journal of Feminist Studies in Religion*, Spring 1990, p. 48.

Chapter 6: Revelation and Connected Knowing

1 I write this with a feeling of near despair with regard to world reactions to the successive African famines. 'Compassion-fatigue' has set in towards 'the famine the world forgot'. The spectacle of death on such a vast scale has failed to change government policies with regard to the Third World. Individual protest and non-governmental agencies can struggle to change the climate of opinion. But without a radical change in our understanding of the meaning of life on earth, in humanity's basic sense of self, the systems which spawn indifference will persist.
2 A. N. Whitehead, *Process and Reality*, Cambridge, Macmillan, 1929; the quotation is from Marjorie Suchocki, *God, Christ, Church: A Practical Guide to Process Theology* (New York, Crossroad, rev. edn 1989), p. 203.
3 I have been influenced here by C. Keller, *From a Broken Web* (Boston, Beacon Press, 1986), chs 4 and 5.
4 ibid., p. 236.
5 Jung, *Psychology of the Child Archetype*; quoted by Keller, p. 237.
6 For the importance of rethinking 'Soulmaking' I am indebted to James Hillman, *Re-visioning Psychology*, New York and San Francisco, Harper & Row, 1975.
7 See ch. 4, n. 13.
8 See ch. 4, n. 6.
9 The concept of empathic knowing has been developed by the Stone Center: see Judith V. Jordan, J. Surrey and A. Kaplan, 'Women and Empathy: Implications for Psychological Development and Psychotherapy' in Judith V. Jordan et al. *Women's Growth in Connection: Writings from the Stone Center*, pp. 21–42; Judith V. Jordan, 'Empathy and Self-Boundaries', in ibid., pp. 67–80.
10 Quoted by Heidegger, *Being and Time*, Oxford, Blackwell, 1962, p. 242. The fable is actually No. 220 of the Fables of Hyginus, and the text is from F. Buchler, *Rheinisches Museum* 41, 1886, p. 5.
11 Anders Nygren, *Eros and Agape*, London, SPCK, 1953.
12 Sara Ruddick, quoted in Mary Field Belenky et al., *Women's Ways of Knowing* (New York, Basic Books, 1986), p. 143.
13 Andrea Nye, *Words of Power: A Feminist Reading of the History of Logic*, New York and London, Routledge, 1990.
14 ibid., pp. 85–102. See also M. Grey, 'The Challenge of Héloise: Language, Truth and Logic Re-visited, *New Blackfriars*, February 1992, pp. 84–9. For Helen Waddell and the connection with Héloise, see

Felicitas Corrigan, *Helen Waddell: a Biography*, London, Victor Gollancz, 1986.

15 Gemma Corradi Fiumara, *The Other Side of Language: A Philosophy of Listening*, London and New York, Routledge, 1990.

16 quoted in Fiumara, p. 3.

17 quoted in Fiumara, p. 8.

18 Fiumara, p. 23.

19 Ruddick, p. 143.

20 Plato, 'Theaetetus', in *The Dialogues of Plato*, Oxford, The Clarendon Press, 1953.

21 quoted in Fiumara, pp. 146–8.

22 The phrase is from the late Nelle Morton, 'The Rising Woman-Consciousness in a Male Language Structure', in *The Journey is Home* (Boston, Beacon Press, 1985), p. 17.

23 Chung Hyun Kyung, *Struggle to be the Sun Again* (London, SCM Press, 1990) p. 39.

24 Don Cupitt, *What is a Story?* London, SCM Press, 1991.

Chapter 7: The Fragility of Divine Communication

1 Elizabeth Behr-Sigel, *The Ministry of Women in the Church* (California, Oakwood, 1991), pp. 19, 94–5.

2 Daphne Hampson, *Theology and Feminism*, Oxford, Blackwell, 1990.

3 Anne-Louise Gilligan and Katherine Zappone, 'Sacraments are Bad for the Health', *The Irish Times*, 21 December 1991.

4 See Catherina Halkes, *Met Miriam is het Begonnen*, Kok, Kampen, 1980; H. Langer, H. Leistner and E. Moltmann-Wendel, *Met Miriam door de Rietzee*, Boxtel, Katholieke Bijbelstichting, 1983.

5 This poem was originally written in the context of a working party on religious education and racism, which met over two years to produce a book on the Church and racism in Britain; See M. Grey and R. Zipfel, *From Barriers to Community*, London, HarperCollins, 1991. The poem tries to keep in tension Miriam as community leader, leading the dance of liberation (Exodus 15.20–1) and Miriam, stricken with leprosy, social outcast (Numbers 12.1–16).

6 Furthermore, as Brian Wren points out, the current stereotypes of masculinity (MAWKI = Masculinism As We Know It) are seriously flawed; see his *What Language Shall I Borrow?* (London, SCM Press, 1989), part 1, 'Masculinity as a Theological Problem'.

7 See M. Grey, 'The Core of our Desire: Re-imaging the Trinity', *Theology*, October 1990, pp. 363–72.

8 ibid., p. 371.

9 M. Suchocki, 'The Unmale God: Reconsidering the Trinity', *Quarterly Review*, Spring 1983, pp. 34–49.

10 Matthew Fox, *The Coming of the Cosmic Christ: The Healing of Mother Earth and the Birth of a Global Renaissance* (San Francisco, Harper & Row, 1988), pp. 133–5.

11 ibid., p. 135.
12 See M. Grey, *Redeeming the Dream*, pp. 95–108.
13 See M. Grey, 'Where Does the Wild Goose Fly To? Seeking a New Theology of Spirit for Feminist Theology?' *New Blackfriars*, February 1991, pp. 89–96.

Chapter 8: God and Evil within a Metaphysic of Connection

1 I also explored this question in the context of the Arthurian legend of Morgan Le Fay in 'The Dark Knowing of Morgan Le Fay' in Teresa Elwes, ed., *Women and Religion*, London, Marshall Pickering, 1992.
2 Fyodor Dostoevsky, *The Brothers Karamazov* (London, Penguin, 1958), p. 287.
3 Eli Wiesel, *The Trial of God*, New York, Random House, 1977. See Dan Cohn-Sherbok, *Holocaust Theology* (London, Marshall, Morgan and Scott, 1989), pp. 92–103.
4 See Rosemary Ruether, *Sexism and God-Talk* (London, SCM Press, 1983), ch. 7.
5 ibid., p. 160.
6 E. Colledge OSA and James Walsh SJ, eds., *Julian of Norwich: Showings* (London, SPCK; New York, Paulist, 1978), p. 23: 'O wretched sin, what are you? You are nothing. For I saw that God is in everything. And when I saw that God had made everything, I did not see you. And when I saw that God does everything that is done, the less and the great, I did not see you . . . And so I am certain that you are nothing . . .'.
7 John Hick, *Evil and the God of Love* (London, Collins, 1968), ch. 13.
8 C. S. Lewis, *A Grief Observed* (London, Faber, 1976), p. 50.
9 Dorothee Soelle, *Suffering* (Philadelphia, Fortress, 1975), p. 32.
10 Rita Nakashima Brock, 'And a Little Child Will Lead us: Christology and Child Abuse', in Rebecca Parker and Carol S. Bohn, eds., *Christianity, Patriarchy and Abuse*, New York, Pilgrim, 1989.
11 Elisabeth Moltmann-Wendel criticizes this and similar interpretations in 'Is there a Feminist Theology of the Cross?' in E. Moltmann-Wendel and J. Moltmann, *His God and Hers*, London, SCM Press, 1991, pp. 87–91. For a systematic feminist christology, see Doris Strahm and Regula Strobel, eds., *Vom Verlangen nach Heilwerden: Christologie in Feministisch-theologischer Sicht*, Fribourg, Editions Exodus, 1991.
12 See report in *The Guardian*, 9 January 1992.
13 Catherine Madsen, 'If God is God She Is Not Nice', *Journal of Feminist Studies in Religion* Spring 1989, pp. 103–5.
14 Helen Waddell, *Peter Abelard* (London, Constable, 1933), p. 103.
15 For example, Nel Noddings, *Women and Evil* (Berkeley, University of California Press, 1989), ch. 2; Rosemary Ruether, 'Dualism and the Nature of Evil in feminist Theology', *Studies in Christian Ethics*, vol. 5, no. 1, pp. 26–39.
16 Despite this prevailing tradition the Orthodox Church preserves a tradition that Mary Magdalen was *isapostolon*, 'equal to the apostles'; see

Notes

George Poulos, in *Ecumenical Decade, 1988–1998: Churches in Solidarity with Women* (Geneva, World Council of Churches), p. 61. Considerable work is being done to recover authentic traditions about Mary Magdalen; see Carla Ricci, *Maria de Magdala e Le Molte Altre*, Naples, D'Auria Editore, 1991; Elizabeth Moltmann-Wendel, *The Women around Jesus* (London, SCM Press, 1982), pp. 61–90.

17 Carl Gustav Jung, *Collected Works*, 9(1):98, quoted in Demeris Wehr, *Jung and Feminism: Liberating Archetypes* (London, Routledge, 1988), p. 106.

18 ibid., p. 110.

19 *The Confessions of St Augustine*, London, Collins, Fontana, 1957, tr. by Sir Tobie Matthew.

20 See Mara Lyn Keller, 'The Eleusinian Mysteries of Demeter and Persephone: Fertility, Sexuality and Rebirth', *Journal of Feminist Studies in Religion* Spring 1988, pp. 27–54.

21 Ernst Becker, *The Denial of Death* (New York, Free Press, 1973), pp. 39–40, quoted in Wehr, *Jung and Feminism*, p. 111.

22 For an exploration of cross-cultural difference in feminist theology see Kristin Metz, 'Passionate Difference: A Working Model for Cross-cultural Communication, *Journal of Feminist Studies in Religion* Spring 1990, pp. 131–51.

23 Mary Daly, *Gyn/Ecology* (Boston, Beacon Press, 1978), pp. 413–14.

24 Wendy Farley, *Tragic Vision and Divine Compassion: A Contemporary Theodicy*, Louisville, KY, Westminster/John Knox Press, 1990.

25 Grace Jantzen, *God's World, God's Body* (London, Darton, Longman and Todd, 1984), p. 101.

26 See C. Keller, *From a Broken Web* (Boston, Beacon Press, 1988), pp. 214–15: 'A Self is a node in the network of world, and in each self is an Eros ensouling the world. The world has heart – where we embrace the Universe as condensed, personified, particularized, in those metaphors of the sacred that inspire us. If we meet God in ourselves, we meet her at the molten core of our heart's desire, ever again energising our courage and our quest.'

27 See above, n. 25.

28 The theme of the fragility of goodness in relation to ethics is explored by Martha Nussbaum in *The Fragility of Goodness: Luck and Ethics in Greek Tragedy and Philosophy*, Cambridge, Cambridge University Press, 1986.

29 Farley, *Tragic Vision*.

30 ibid., p. 72.

31 ibid., p. 84.

32 ibid., p. 93.

33 Sharon Welch, *A Feminist Ethic of Risk* (Minneapolis, Fortress, 1990), pp. 154–5.

34 Susan Thistlethwaite, *Sex, Race and God: Christian Feminism in Black and White*, London, Geoffrey Chapman, 1990.

35 Colledge and Walsh, p. 23.

36 *Confessions*, tr. Matthew, p. 181: 'That evil, then, of which I sought whence it was, is not any substance, because, if it were a substance, it

would be good. . . . Therefore I saw, and that clearly, that all things which thou madest were good, and there are no substances at all which thou didst not make.'

37 C. S. Lewis, *The Great Divorce*, London, Collins, 1971.
38 Elaine Scarry, *The Body in Pain*, (Oxford and New York, Oxford University Press, 1985), pp. 60ff.
39 ibid., p. 137.

Chapter 9: The Church: Permanently Marginal or Leaven for Change?

1 Sharon Welch, *Communities of Resistance and Solidarity* (New York, Orbis, 1985), p. 54.
2 Morris West, *The Clowns of God* (London, Hodder & Stoughton, 1981), pp. 423–5.
3 For the early history of Women-Church see Mary-Jo Weaver, *New Catholic Women: A Contemporary Challenge to Traditional Religious Authority* (San Francisco, Harper & Row, 1985), pp. 132–6.
4 ibid., p. 133.
5 Rosemary Ruether, *Women-Church: Theology and Practice* (New York, Harper & Row, 1985), p. 72.
6 Riet Bons-Storm, 'Pastoraat buiten de muur van het Vaderhuis', Inaugural Lecture, University of Groningen, 29 January 1991.
7 Elisabeth Schüssler Fiorenza, *In Memory of Her* (London, SCM Press, 1983), pp. 105ff.
8 See Riet Bons-Storm and Diana Vernooij, eds., *Beweging in Macht: Vrouw Kerk in Nederland?* Kampen, Kok, 1991.
9 See *Waterwheel*, the quarterly newsletter of the Women's Alliance for Theology, Ethics and Ritual, Summer 1990. In 'Defining "Women-Church"', Mary Hunt writes: 'My definition of Women-Church is a global, ecumenical movement made up of local feminist base-communities and justice-seeking friends who engage in sacrament and solidarity.' As regards the theology of Women-Church: 'We do not seek a creed nor a set of dogmas . . . Rather, with our feminist brothers and our children we seek to live out a theology of "mutual relation" . . . and a praxis of radical love.' See also 'Spiral not Schism: Women-Church as Church', *Religion and Intellectual Life* Fall 1989, pp. 89–92.
10 Chung Hyun Kyung, *Struggle to be the Sun Again*, London, SCM Press, 1990.
11 Chung Hyun Kyung, *Come, Holy Spirit*, WCC Seventh Assembly, Canberra, 8 February 1991, document no. PL 3.3.
12 Mercy Amba Oduyoye, *Who Will Roll the Stone Away? The Ecumenical Decade of the Churches in Solidarity with Women* (Geneva, WCC, Risk Publications, 1990), p. 14.
13 Quoted in ibid., p. 41.
14 For The Catholic Women's Network see *Network: The Journal of the Catholic Women's Network*, a quarterly publication. Women in Theology

(WIT) also produces a quarterly mailing. Both of these contain a rich mixture of reviews, articles, reporting and announcing of events, rituals, campaigns, as well as playing an important part in building community, 'weaving new connections' and (in the case of the Catholic Women's Network) participating in the political struggle in Church and society.

15 For the St Hilda's Community see *Women Included* (London, SPCK, 1991), a collection of the prayers and liturgies of the community since it began meeting in 1987. For the story of the community see 'God and Women', *The Independent Magazine*, 2 November 1991, pp. 38–41. For an idea of the public reaction which *Women Included* evoked, see Ruth Gledhill, 'Ladies and the Name of the Lord', *The Times*, 23 October 1991, p. 13.

16 Christian Aid and CAFOD – the two largest and most well-known Church non-governmental aid agencies – have become increasingly aware of the problems of women in the struggle for justice in the Third World and have tried to make this a prominent part of their educational programmes. Janet Morley's new book is a shining example of this: *Bread of Tomorrow: Praying with the World's Poor*, London, Christian Aid and SPCK, 1992.

17 For the history of the struggle within the Church of England see especially Monica Furlong, *A Dangerous Delight* (London, SPCK, 1991), as well as *Chrysalis*, bulletin of the Movement for the Ordination of Women.

18 The intuition that 'The Spirit *is* the Church' (but *not* the reverse – 'The Church is the Spirit'!) has three grounds: the first is the theology of Luke, whose special insight it was that the work of the Spirit is inseparable from the birth and growth of Christian community; second, from the baptismal credal expressions of the early Church, in which the expression of belief in the Trinity was also belief in, and commitment to the Church; and third, from the conviction, expressed by Martin Buber, among others, that human nature is relational, and only in the acknowledgement of mutuality is the presence of God experienced. See John V. Taylor, *The Go-Between God*, London, Collins, 1974; T. J. Gorringe, *Discerning Spirit – A Theology of Revelation* (London, SCM Press, 1990), ch. 5.

19 See James Mackey, *The Christian Experience of God as Trinity*, London, SCM Press, 1983.

20 Leonardo Boff, *The Maternal Face of God: The Feminine and its Religious Expressions*, Brazil, Petropolis, 1979; London, Collins, 1989); see the discussion on Congar's (and others') suggestions on the Spirit as the femininity of God in Sarah Coakley, 'Femininity and the Holy Spirit', in Monica Furlong, ed., *Mirror to the Church* (London, SPCK, 1988), pp. 124–35.

21 See my criticism in M. Grey, 'Reclaiming Mary: A Task for Feminist Theology', *The Way*, October 1989, pp. 334–40.

22 This is the (Dutch) title of a collection of essays on the Holy Spirit dedicated to Catherina Halkes on her retirement: *Zij waait waarheen zij wil: Opstellen over de Geest*, eds. Riet Bons Storm, Denise Dijk, Annelies van Heijst et al., Baarn, Ten Have, 1986.

23 See M. Grey, 'Where does the Wild Goose Fly To?' *New Blackfriars* February 1991, pp. 89–96.

24 This dimension of the Spirit rests ultimately on the Gospel of John: 'When the Spirit of truth comes, he will guide you into all the truth; for he will not speak on his own authority, but whatever he hears, he will speak, and he will declare to you the things that are to come. He will glorify me, for he will take what is mine and declare it to you. All that the Father has is mine; therefore I said that he will take what is mine and declare it to you' (John 16.13–15).

25 See Taylor, *The Go-Between God.*

26 Both Rita Brock and Susan Thistlethwaite criticize feminist christologies which, in an attempt to develop a christology of mutual relation, are insensitive to the fact that they do so in opposition to Judaism. They cite Judith Plaskow as making it abundantly clear that the Jesus Movement was a movement within Judaism, and as asserting that white feminists '. . . have not found a consistent way to talk about Jesus that is in harmony with their concerns about Jewish–Christian relations'. See Judith Plaskow, 'Feminist Anti-Judaism: Some New Considerations, *Crosscurrents* Fall 1978, p. 25; Susan Thistlethwaite, *Sex, Race and God* (London, Geoffrey Chapman, 1990), pp. 94–108; Rita Brock, *Journeys by Heart* (New York, Crossroad, 1988), pp. 6–14. Thistlethwaite finds that Brock has avoided anti-semitism by grounding messianic, relational power in community. But she has still (over-optimistically) stressed connectedness to the detriment of difference, destruction and evil. The debate goes on . . . .

27 '. . . this points to a much closer relationship between God/World/ Spirit/Church than traditional theology has supposed. From both Process theology and from the recent work of Feminist Theologians . . . has come the organic link between the being of God and the cosmos. . . . It does flesh out the travail of creation as also the travail of God. It does give content to the suffering of God. If the birds, sing no more, sky and earth are polluted, certain possibilities of God are lost. In a certain sense "God has died" as parts of God's Body have been destroyed by humanity's greed.' M. Grey, 'Does Feminist Theology have a Vision for Christian Church?' *Louvain Studies* 16, 1991, pp. 27–40.

28 This is explored beautifully in Taylor, *The Go-Between God,* ch. 1.

29 Fiorenza, *In Memory of Her,* pp. xiii–xxv.

30 Matthew Fox, *The Coming of the Cosmic Christ,* (San Francisco, Harper & Row, 1988), pt 1 'Your mother is dying – a crucifixion story for our times'; pt 2, 'Mysticism, a resurrection story for our times'.

31 See Fiona Bowie and Oliver Davies, eds., *Hildegarde of Bingen: An Anthology* (London, SPCK; New York, Crossroad, 1990); the bibliography is very helpful.

32 *Redeeming the Dream,* pp. 63–83.

Notes

Chapter 10: A Revelation Story for our Times?

1 The torrent of literature on Glastonbury, Avalon and Arthurian legends is too overwhelming to cite. Glastonbury 'spirituality' at this moment includes a feminist re-telling of the legends, the increasing popularity of the Grail motif, New Age spirituality and Goddess spirituality, as well as an increasing quantity of 'fantasy' literature. For a collection of articles on recent, evolving reflection on the old sources, see John Matthews, ed., *The Household of the Grail*, Wellingborough, The Aquarian Press, 1990; R. J. Stewart, ed., *Merlin and Woman: The Book of the Second Merlin Conference*, London and New York, The Blandford Press, 1988.

2 For the theme of the banishing of the Goddess religion see Marion Zimmer Bradley, *The Mists of Avalon*, London, Michael Joseph, 1983.

3 In all the works I have consulted for this chapter, the only interpretation of the Book of Revelation which I have found inspirational is Catherine Keller, 'Der Frau in der Wüste: ein Feministisch-theologischer Midrasch zu Offb. 12', *Evang. Theol.* 50, No. 5, pp. 414–32.

4 See John M. Court, *Myth and History in the Book of Revelation*, London, SPCK, 1974.

5 See Caitlin Matthews, *Sophia – Goddess of Wisdom: the Divine Feminine From Black Goddess to World Soul*, London, HarperCollins, Mandala, 1991.

6 For resources on Psyche and Eros, see C. Keller, *From a Broken Web* (Boston, Beacon Press, 1986), ch. 4; C. S. Lewis, *Till We Have Faces: A Myth Re-Told*, London, Collins, 1974; Carol White, *Eros and Psyche*, The International Grail Centre, De Tiltenberg, The Netherlands, 1986; James Hillman, *Re-Visioning Psychology*, New York and San Francisco, Harper & Row, 1975.

Index

Abelard, Peter 88, 107, 153n, 155n
Aeneas and Dido 70–1, 152n
Aquinas, St Thomas 11, 12
Arachne, Spider Goddess 60–1, 150n
Aristotelian logic 83
Augustine, St: and theodicy 103, 105; and spiritual struggle 109, 156n; and will 113; and sin 117, 156–7n
Avalon, vale of 137–9

Barclay, William 36
Barnes, Albert 36
Barth, Karl 75
Bateson, Gregory and the ecological self 77
Becker, Ernst 109–10, 156n
Behr-Sigel, Elizabeth 93, 94, 154n
Benavides, Marta 66, 151n
Bernard of Clairvaux, St 43
Bernadette of Lourdes, St 21–2
Berry, Thomas 74, 151n
Boff, Leonardo 128, 158n
Bons-Storm, Riet 123, 157n, 158n
Brock, Rita Nakashima 60; and child abuse 105, 155n; on Christology and anti-Judaism 150n, 159n
Buber, Martin 12, 74, 146n
Buddhist images 77

Care, Myth of 87–8, 153n
'caring knowing' 87–8
Cassandra 49–56, 84, 111, 133
Catholic Women's Network 126, 157n
Cheney, Jim 79, 153n
Chung Hyun Kyung 55–6, 65, 91, 125, 143, 150n; and Canberra 127–8
Clinebell, Howard 86, 150n
Coakley, Sarah 158n
Cone, James 19, 146n
Constitution of Second Vatican Council on Revelation (*Dei Verbum*) 1
Cox, Harvey 2–3, 145n
Cupitt, Don 92, 154n

Daly, Mary 42, 93, 148n, 149n
deconstruction 145n
Dei Verbum see Constitution of Second Vatican Council
Delphi, Temple of Apollo at 81–2
Dido and Aeneas 70–1, 152n
Dillard, Annie 79–80, 106, 153n
Dostoevsky, Fyodor: and female subjectivity 30–2; and *The Brothers Karamazov* 102, 155n
Dulles, Avery and *Models of Revelation* 17–21, 24, 28–9, 146n

Echlin, Edward 74, 152n
Eliot, George (Marian Evans):

Middlemarch 20, 145n; and 'epiphany of connection' 61; *Romola* 46–7, 149n

'empathic knowing' 87, 153n

epistemology of connected knowing 84–92 *passim*, 110–12; and Asian women 91–2

Eros and Psyche 160n

Esquivel, Julia 126, 157n

Farley, Wendy 115–16, 156n

Fiorenza, Elisabeth Schüssler 62, 151n; and Women-Church 123–4, 157n; and prophetic anointing 132, 159n; and the periodicisation of history 146n

Fiumara, Gemma Corradi 89–91, 154n; and mysticism 134–5, 159n

Fox-Genovese, Elizabeth and individualism 34, 148n

Furlong, Monica 158n

Gilligan, Anne-Louise 94, 154n

Gilligan, Carol 70–1, 152n

God: as Trinity 99–100, 154n; and transcendence/immanence 113–14; and power of compassion 115–16, 156n; and theodicy 101–19

Grail, Legend of 137–41, 145n, 160n; *see also* Perceval

Hagar 15–16, 97, 146n

Halkes, Catherina 61, 151n, 154n, 158n

Hampson, Daphne 93, 154n

Heidegger: and Myth of Care 86, 153n; and logos 89

Helfta, Gertrude of 21

Héloise 88, 107, 153–4n, 155n

Heyward, Carter 59, 150n, 113

Hick, John 103, 104, 155n

Hilda, St, Community of 126, 158n

Hildegarde of Bingen 21–2, 147n; as bearer of revelation 98; and mysticism 135, 159n

Hunt, Mary and Women-Church 125, 157n

Jantzen, Grace 113–14, 156nn; immanence and transcendence 14, 156n

Julian of Norwich 103, 155n; and sin 117

Jung, Carl Gustav 108–9, 156n

Keller, Catherine: and metaphor of connection 59, 60, 150n; and connected self 68, 74, 76, 151n, 152n; and immanence 113, 156n; and the Book of Revelation 141–3, 160n

Kristeva, Julia 32, 75; and 'Living the Sacrifice' 37–46, 148n, 149n

Kwon-in-Sook 55–6

Lewis, C.S. 104, 155n; and sin 117, 157n

Locke 88, 89

Logos: in confrontation with the Holy Fool and Sophia 5–9, 81–4; and logocentric culture, 69, 90–1

Macy, Joanna 77, 152n

Madsen, Catherine 155n

Magic Flute, The and demonization of the mother 109

Martyrs, Jesuit of El Salvador 113

Mary, Mother of Jesus 22, 28, 32–3; and *Mulieris Dignitatem* 36–7; and Julia Kristeva 42–6, 149n; as *virgo intacta* 108; and the feminine dimension of God 128, 158n; and links with the Goddess 147n

Mary Magdalen, symbolism of 108, 155n, 156n

Metz, Jean-Baptist 116

Miriam 94–7, 154n

Moltmann-Wendel, Elisabeth 155n

Morrison, Toni 64, 151n

Movement for the Ordination of Women 126

Mozart *see The Magic Flute*

mysticism: and Hildegarde of Bingen 135, 159n; and *Redeeming the Dream* 135, 159n; as epiphanies of connection 136; *see also* Matthew Fox

myth 1–3, 5–9; of Demeter and Persephone 109, 156n; of Grail: *see* Perceval; and Jungian personality theory 108–9, 156n; of Odysseus and Penelope 69–70; *see also* Logos and Sophia

Neu, Dianne and Women-Church 125, 157n

Nye, Andrea 88, 153n

Oduyoye, Mercy Amba 125–7, 157n

Otto, Rudolph 75

Page, Ruth and ambiguity 152n

Perceval: as The Holy Fool 2–4, 145nn; in encounter with Logos and Sophia 5–9, 10, 81–4; and Grail legends 137–41, 160n

Plaskow, Judith and anti-Judaism in Christian theology 159n

Plato: and Timaeus 38; and Theaetetus 90–1, 154n; and Socrates 90–1

postmodernism 10, 145n

Primavesi, Anne 61, 86, 151n

Psyche 141, 160n

Revelation, the Book of 140–3

Rich, Adrienne 11, 14, 35, 57, 78, 88, 146n, 147n, 150n, 153n

Ruddick, Sara and 'maternal knowing' 87–8, 90, 153n

Ruether, Rosemary Radford 113, 114; and Women-Church 123, 157n

Sartre, Jean-Paul and female sexuality 108

Savaranamutti, Morani 105

Scarry, Elaine 72, 157n

sin as structural de-creation 117–18

Socrates and 'midwife thinking' 83, 90–1, 154n

Soelle, Dorothee 104, 155n

Sophia: in encounters with Logos and Perceval 1–4, 5–9, 81–4, 85, 139–43; as the woman in the Book of Revelation 141–3, 160n

Spirit, the Holy: and Chung Hyun Kyung 127–8, 157n; as the Church 128, 158n; as our mother 128, 158n; as energy of connection 129–34, 158n, 159n; and annunciation 131–2

Steiner, George 70, 152n

Swinburne, Richard 103

Suchocki, Marjorie 99, 154n

Von Morstein, Petra 55, 149–150n

Waddell, Helen 107, 155n

Walker, Alice 61, 63–5, 151n

Ward, Mary 98

Wehr, Demaris 108–9, 156n

Welch, Sharon: and 'dangerous memory' 116, 156n; and liberation theology 120, 157n

West, Morris 120–1, 157n

Whitehead, Alfred North 74, 85, 153n

Wiesel, Eli 102, 155n

Wolf, Christa 49, 149n, 150n

Women-Church 122–7, 157n

Woman and Faith Movement (Vrouw en Geloof Beweging) 124–5, 157n

Women in Theology 126, 157–8n

Zappone, Katherine 94, 154n